Praise f

M000167352

As a society, we are long overdue in reimagining the social contract in light of contemporary realities and mega trends. The events of 2020 have laid bare how damaging it is to continue to allow antiquated systems and business models to persist. *Beyond Good* is the book leaders and change makers (from all sectors – private, public and non-profit) need to read as we co-create new solutions and forge a path to a more inclusive social contract that allows all to live with dignity, security, and purpose. RAMSEY ALWIN, PRESIDENT AND CHIEF EXECUTIVE OFFICER, NCOA

Beyond Good is far from a typical business book. It is a thought-provoking read that articulates simply and clearly the principles that everyone can – and should – apply across all aspects of life, in the workplace and beyond. Making the world a fairer place is in our hands, and *Beyond Good* inspires you to strive for it, for the common good. TANYA ANDREASYAN, MANAGING DIRECTOR AND EDITOR-IN-CHIEF, *FINTECH FUTURES*

Look no further for a roadmap of the central challenges facing civil society at the intersection of technology, ethics, and economic inequality. *Beyond Good* reimagines what progress looks like within an empathy and inclusion context, and provides new insights into one of the most enduring social challenges: how can technology build equitable and sustainable economic prosperity? *Beyond Good* is the best place to start for an answer, because it forces us to rethink how innovation can be part of the solution. SCOTT ASTRADA, ADJUNCT PROFESSOR OF LAW AT GEORGETOWN UNIVERSITY CENTER, AND DIGITAL CIVIL SOCIETY FELLOW, STANFORD UNIVERSITY, CENTER ON PHILANTHROPY AND CIVIL SOCIETY

We need more books like this. Theodora Lau and Bradley Leimer have clearly done their homework and used their lockdown time well. As we see more companies aiming to deliver sustainable and ethical services, this book, full of positive and practical real-world examples, aims to educate and inform us that it is possible to achieve results that are beyond good. SIMON COCKING, CHIEF EDITOR, *IRISH TECH NEWS*

Theodora Lau and Bradley Leimer provide a sweeping look at the trends that define our changing world, challenging leaders in financial services to direct their inherent power to shape a more equitable and empathetic global economy. CATHERINE HARVEY, US ECONOMIC POLICY EXPERT

From financial inclusion to gender equality, from empathetic leadership to inclusive entrepreneurship, *Beyond Good* covers a wide spectrum of socially conscious strategies for business leaders. Abundance of detailed research and insights delivered with conviction makes it a compelling read. Some books leave us with something to think about. In contrast, *Beyond Good* will stay with us for a very long time by providing a roadmap to a more equal and sustainable world for generations to come. A must-read for every socially conscious mind. ARUN KRISHNAKUMAR, PARTNER, DELPHOS INTERNATIONAL

Bradley Leimer and Theodora Lau smash through the boundaries of traditional business models, and expose us to a new purposeful, inclusive and empathetic world where everyone can genuinely still win together for the common good. *Beyond Good* will compel you to consider the real future of business, inspire you to be a part of it and to take action in your communities to make it happen. An absolutely essential read. PAUL LOBERMAN, CHIEF PRODUCT OFFICER, UNTIED

I love Theodora Lau's and Bradley Leimer's *Beyond Good* and recommend it to everyone in the start-up world wholeheartedly. We all should aim to advance technology and help its involved participants to fulfil the ultimate goal to drive the purpose-driven business technology revolution. SPIROS MARGARIS, VENTURE CAPITALIST AND ADVISOR, MARGARIS VENTURES

Beyond Good is a timely and essential read for global financial service executives. Theodora Lau and Bradley Leimer persuasively show that now – more than ever — is the time for business leaders to play a crucial role in tackling our most pressing societal challenges and engage in significant commercial opportunities that do well by doing good. This book is an invaluable resource for all those inspired to harness technology innovation to build a fairer and more inclusive financial system. SARAH MOGENSTERN, VENTURE PARTNER, FLOURISH VENTURES

Acting upon a sense of broader purpose is instinctual. We evolved with basic instincts to band together and act in the common good. The common economic models in play just don't pass the smell test as sustainable. *Beyond Good* deconstructs and then reconstructs a better way forward. There is a strong theme of interconnectivity throughout this book that makes a strong case for empathy and awareness of how our choices and strategies never happen in a vacuum. We can choose to forge a path that leaves in its wake a positive impact, or we can choose a path of zero-sum gain. Throughout this read, I was frequently able to make connections to tangible ways that I and our organization can coalesce around a better way forward. CURT QUEYROUZE, PRESIDENT, TAB BANK

Beyond Good reminds us that behind every company doing well are passionate people who are doing good. Today's seemingly impossible challenges can be met by us, if we're brave enough to act. For those in financial services, the call to action is clear: when you create a strong culture that leads with empathy and pair it with today's technology, you are uniquely positioned to make a positive difference. You can lead with purpose and build your own success! MATTHEW SEKOL, INDUSTRY EXECUTIVE, CAPITAL MARKETS, MICROSOFT

There are many themes of the 21st century that resonate in *Beyond Good* – a more inclusive society, addressing the climate emergency, creating a better world and more – all enabled by technology, governmental and financial market change. This book is an essential guide to rethinking our world for the good of society and the planet. In other words, beyond good to beautiful. Who could ignore that? Thoroughly recommended. CHRIS SKINNER, CHIEF EXECUTIVE OFFICER, THE FINANSER LTD

An inspiring meditation on the many ways we can take action to make a mark on the world. Reading *Beyond Good* will leave you wanting to be an empathetic leader who champions efforts that address big societal problems, like economic inequalities and ageism. As Theodora Lau and Bradley Leimer write: Our work means something more than a value exchange for money. MARY WISNIEWSKI, BANKING EDITOR, *BANKRATE*

Beyond Good

*How technology is leading
a purpose-driven business revolution*

Theodora Lau

Bradley Leimer

Kogan Page
INSPIRE

Publisher's note
Every possible effort has been made to ensure that the information contained in this book is accurate at the time of going to press, and the publishers and authors cannot accept responsibility for any errors or omissions, however caused. No responsibility for loss or damage occasioned to any person acting, or refraining from action, as a result of the material in this publication can be accepted by the editor, the publisher or the authors.

First published in Great Britain and the United States in 2021 by Kogan Page Limited

Apart from any fair dealing for the purposes of research or private study, or criticism or review, as permitted under the Copyright, Designs and Patents Act 1988, this publication may only be reproduced, stored or transmitted, in any form or by any means, with the prior permission in writing of the publishers, or in the case of reprographic reproduction in accordance with the terms and licences issued by the CLA. Enquiries concerning reproduction outside these terms should be sent to the publishers at the undermentioned addresses:

2nd Floor, 45 Gee Street	122 W 27th St, 10th Floor	4737/23 Ansari Road
London	New York, NY 10001	Daryaganj
EC1V 3RS	USA	New Delhi 110002
United Kingdom		India

www.koganpage.com

Kogan Page books are printed on paper from sustainable forests.

© Theodora Lau and Bradley Leimer, 2021

The rights of Theodora Lau and Bradley Leimer to be identified as the authors of this work have been asserted by them in accordance with the Copyright, Designs and Patents Act 1988.

This material is a collection of the principles of *Beyond Good* as exemplified by individuals, leaders, business models, foundations, private/public ventures, and businesses profiled in this book. They do not necessarily represent any of the brands or individuals we spoke with during the creation of the book, but are the collective inspiration of what we saw in action during the course of researching and writing this material.

ISBNs

Hardback	978 1 78966 731 8
Paperback	978 1 78966 729 5
Ebook	978 1 78966 730 1

British Library Cataloguing-in-Publication Data

A CIP record for this book is available from the British Library.

Library of Congress Control Number

2020952022

Typeset by Integra Software Services, Pondicherry
Print production managed by Jellyfish
Printed and bound by CPI Group (UK) Ltd, Croydon CR0 4YY

This book is dedicated to our families and friends, and all those who work tirelessly to make the world a better place.

Contents

About the authors

Theodora Lau

Theodora Lau is the Founder of Unconventional Ventures. She is a public speaker, writer and adviser, whose work seeks to spark innovation to improve consumer health and financial wellbeing. She focuses on developing and growing an ecosystem of financial institutions, corporates, entrepreneurs and venture capitalists to better address the unmet needs of consumers, with a focus on women and minority founders. She co-hosts One Vision, a podcast on innovation and FinTech.

Bradley Leimer

Bradley Leimer, Co-Founder of Unconventional Ventures, writes and speaks about banking and technology, and advises startups, accelerators and major corporates. He is the former Head of Innovation at Banco Santander, and led data-driven marketing strategies and digital-technology programmes within regional banks and community-focused credit unions. He co-hosts One Vision, a podcast on innovation and FinTech.

About Unconventional Ventures

Unconventional Ventures provides consulting services to drive innovation to improve systematic financial wellbeing. We connect founders to funders, provide mentorship to entrepreneurs, strategic advisory services to a broad set of corporates, and broaden opportunities for diversity within the ecosystem. Our belief is that anyone with great ideas should have a chance to succeed. We work with banking clients, FinTech startups, conference and media organizers and technology firms. Our approach is to help these players navigate, contextualize and diversify their business models in order to be prepared for the changes to the broader financial-services landscape.

Foreword

The invitation to write the foreword to this book was extended – and accepted – under vastly different circumstances from those that we are experiencing today. Even in the old version of the world that was not living through a worldwide pandemic and the deepest global recession since the Second World War, Theo and Bradley's vision was compelling – to create a book inviting and inspiring business leaders to play an even bigger role than before in solving society's most pressing challenges. And to use the digital revolution happening in the financial-services sector to show how the purposeful application of technology can be the catalyst for greater social inclusion and equity.

I happily signed on to Theo and Bradley's project because I, too, felt that the urgency for change was clear even before 2020. In the midst of the longest economic expansion in US history, millions of workers experienced deteriorating financial and physical health. And while global inequality between countries was decreasing and tens of millions of people had moved out of deepest poverty, in-country inequality was reaching historic levels, undermining social cohesion and dangerously increasing political polarization.

Enter 2020, and coronavirus, and the global lockdowns implemented to contain it revealed just how deep and systemic the fault lines of inequality lay, and also how interdependent we all are. If the call for the business sector to lean into social purpose was growing before the pandemic, changing circumstances spurred a sea-change.

Overnight, the dominant narratives of the business sector's leading role in driving economic growth were tempered by a new-found respect for essential workers and the reality that an economy fuelled by consumption was capable of freefall when workers with volatile cash flow, living pay cheque to pay cheque, lacked the means to keep demand strong.

To the degree that the economy has stayed tenable, much of the success can be attributed to the ways in which technology has facilitated everything from remote work to tele-health to digital payments. Already we are seeing evidence that countries that prioritized digital financial inclusion and interoperability with government safety net programmes are experiencing greater economic resilience and faster recoveries.

Conversely, the many failures contributing to human suffering – and disproportionately harming Black, Indigenous and People of Colour (BIPOC) communities – are evidence of how much work is ahead of us, and how critical it is that leaders in all sectors centre our most ambitious and innovative thinking on solving for core problems. When solved, these solutions will provide households with the financial security, dignity and tools to be resilient and capable of contributing to a full economic recovery.

As with so many things in our society right now, this book raises provocative questions, and refreshingly, it doesn't pretend to have all the answers. That is the work we must do together.

Beyond Good is an important companion to other work emerging right now, centred on the margins and talking about the technical and structural-opportunity horizon that we must aim for.

Read it because there is much to be inspired by. Read it because there is a lot of work ahead of us. Read it because we are at an inflection point where business leadership matters and time is of the essence.

Ida Rademacher, Vice President, Aspen Institute and
Executive Director, Aspen Financial Security Program
October 2020

Introduction

But if you want to be a true professional, you will do something outside yourself, something to repair tears in your community, something to make life a little better for people less fortunate than you.[1] JUSTICE RUTH BADER GINSBURG

We didn't start the fire

This is not intended to be a regular business book. We aren't planning to spoon-feed you someone else's dilemma, celebrate the art of any particular war, show you how to be any form of agile, help you go from good to great or ask you to lean in. We regard this book as a guide to the future, a map for exploring new areas you may not often visit or a box you may be too intimidated to open. This book is about rapidly changing demographics and a growing revolution impacting every business model, a planet filled with resonant voices and data points too often glossed over. This isn't about the pledges of progress made in Davos, the policies of

Brussels, Beijing or Washington, DC, or boardroom debates across cities filled with light shows at night. This is the start of an important conversation about the future, a better future, one where we purposely choose to consider how best to fulfil the needs and aspirations of every individual within every community.

This book is about a more inclusive tomorrow, where we imagine a greater sense of the common good, a deeper sense of corporate responsibility. This is about a paradigm shift within our social contract, one that begins and centres around the access and optimization of financial services through technology that cascades across other industries. This is about a new economic reality, one that doesn't get discussed nearly enough. These changes are not looming, they are already here, and their impact on our society is only growing. This catalyst for change is already being felt on the equivalent of Main Street on every continent. Its impact is finally starting to challenge the thinking of corporations and those lucky few currently occupying the corner offices of New York City, London, Hong Kong and Singapore.

By exploring the stories behind the data, we hope to inspire you to take action. Through the activities and aspirations of those already making an impact on the front lines, we hope you find solace that you are not alone in thinking differently about the future, having a desire for action and wanting the ability to change what tomorrow may bring. As we further investigate how we can embed empathy within the enterprise, we will think about ways in which we can work to improve our own community, our society and our increasingly connected world.

A place called hope

One of the most essential elements of being human is the feeling of hope. We like to think that the future will be better, that what we do during our lifetime matters, that we are part of something bigger than ourselves. When we are younger, life is, in most cases, far less complex; responsibilities tend to be fewer, and hope and optimism easier to grasp. What do you want to do when you grow up? What type of impact do you want your life to have? While these are seemingly straightforward questions, answering them is fraught with an array of possibilities that prompts some serious contemplation, especially for adults. But ask a young child this question, and it becomes simpler. The child's answer will most likely be filled with optimism, a sense of hope that, whatever they choose to do, they will surely help other people.

We must continue to nourish this sense of optimism as our society changes, as both emerging technologies and shifting business models shape our sense of belonging, cement our sense of personal responsibility towards others, and impact the choices we make in our life. We must expect the same from every element of society, every corner of every community and the formation of every enterprise. It is in this light that we call for a new social contract and a new methodology to measure the value of the enterprise.

Here's to the dreamers, the contrarians, the drivers of change, the brokers of trust, those that challenge business models and intentions, our corporate rebels, the Sherpas that connect old and new, the silent but impactful, those who think differently, and every one of you that works every day to create a more inclusive society that leads us to an even better future.

Join us on this journey of purpose – to a place called hope.

CHAPTER ONE

Changing tides

Change will not come if we wait for some other person or if we wait for some other time. We are the ones we've been waiting for. We are the change that we seek.[1] BARACK OBAMA

From good to beyond good

In his influential book, *Good to Great*,[2] Jim Collins developed a compelling argument as to why some companies move from being good performers – or even mediocre ones – to becoming great companies built to last. Collins and his team of researchers reviewed the stock performance of 1,435 companies over a 40-year period. They profiled 11 companies in more depth, focusing on several key areas that led to their success. Collins demonstrated that it's critical to get the right people on the bus – the right leaders to drive the business – as well as getting those off the bus who are not contributing to the bottom line.

The book found it vital to have those top performers focused on the greatest opportunities as these leaders established their 'hedgehog' – the defensible core business about which they were deeply passionate, could be the best in the world at, and which drove their central economic engine. The 11 'great' companies that Collins identified included brands such as Abbott Labs, the now online-only Circuit City, Gillette (subsequently bought by Procter & Gamble), Philip Morris, Walgreens and the now scandal-ridden Wells Fargo. As the book reviewed these companies, the importance of leadership finding their BHAG (Big Hairy Audacious Goal) and 'confronting the brutal facts' about their business model became clear, as did their ongoing spotlight on market-driven performance. The book, written shortly after the dotcom implosion, seemed appropriately focused on value, profitability and measured growth during a recovering global business environment.

Another important area that Collins identified and one that would become synonymous with business lexicons written since, such as *Zero to One*[3] by Peter Thiel, was the exploitation of the business model's flywheel, especially in regard to the accelerant that unique business ideas combined with technology can provide. While *Good to Great* continues to influence business leaders today – more than 300,000 copies sell each year – is it time for us to revisit these lessons with a different lens? Should business leaders develop a different kind of centralized model that concurrently considers more deeply the externalities of the communities they serve?

Many societal changes and business-model iterations have transpired since his book was published in 2001, and while Collins and his research teams have written several updates to *Good to Great* (including *Great By Choice*),[4] it does feel as though we should have moved beyond stock performance as the primary barometer of both leadership success and executive compensation by now – given the renewed focus on issues such as diversity, climate change and sustainable investment.

Surely the recent decades of technology-driven business models from Silicon Valley, London and other centres of venture capital have defined 'greatness' differently. And then again, perhaps not. The vast majority of global startups remain private for years of early growth and don't have the scrutiny of public markets – this is indeed the very model for venture-driven teams. Yet startups often follow the amazingly similar path of traditionally created businesses whose aim is to attain market share and growth at all costs through creating their business flywheel. While profitability has been less frequently achieved, securing a significant financial exit remains the focus for many founders and their investors. We can see this in nearly every investment sector and in nearly every geography. So, what has really changed?

Startup business models offer similarities to the success that Collins and his team celebrated. The idea of creating a competitive 'moat' to protect a business's greatest asset – that which is most unassailable to competitors – isn't different from creating the hedgehog that Collins espouses. The concept of becoming lean or agile or moving fast and breaking things doesn't differ greatly from the aggressive efficiency seen at Wells Fargo, well before companies like Facebook even existed or when *Good to Great* was published. The challenges that venture-funded unicorns – privately held startups with a value of over $1 billion – also help create are not inherently different from the impact of traditional non-venture-driven businesses. Even as venture-capital-driven business models have seemingly changed the way we think about how businesses are formed, funded and evolved, we must still ask the question – is that all?

Regardless of the title of the business book, the concepts feel the same; only the names have changed. The purpose of the business model is really at the heart of this discussion. The prevailing narrative leaves us wanting more. Why hasn't our global business culture moved on from focusing on shareholders to a deeper concern for a broader set of stakeholders? How do we begin to measure – and more importantly value – this alternative version of success, one that is not purely based on market performance and profit?

We must start connecting the value of both the positive and negative outcomes that corporations create to the long-term viability of the broader society. Business leaders from all industries must be part of refining and redefining their business outcomes to provide more shared benefits. This is the moment to develop a new social contract between businesses and the communities that they have the privilege to serve.

The role of the enterprise, both big and small, has experienced little change over the past two centuries – but it's now time to expect just that. When Scottish economist Adam Smith published *An Inquiry into the Nature and Causes of the Wealth of Nations*[5] in 1776, he introduced the idea of the invisible hand. The basis of his belief was that 'free individuals operating in a free economy, making decisions, primarily focused on their own self-interest, logically take actions that result in benefiting society as a whole – even though such beneficial results were not the specific focus or intent of those actions.'[6] Smith, considered the founder of modern economics, propagated the idea that government intervention and regulation of the economy was neither necessary nor beneficial, and that the actions of individuals (and businesses) would eventually benefit society and, therefore, the common good. But that's rarely how individuals, corporations or our global economy really seem to work. This is why we continue to see growing forms of inequality and far too many exclusionary business practices that exacerbate this imbalance.

Given this context, how can we redefine what 'good to great' companies really are? Perhaps we can redefine them simply as acting 'beyond great' – going beyond profit and preservation – to a model focused on doing more good in society by creating value for every stakeholder. Let's start by showing you what *Beyond Good* means in practice and ways in which different industries are demonstrating a new sense of purpose.

It only takes a spark

Even a small spark can ignite a revolution. We've seen this throughout human history, as different political events, social movements, demographic tides and economic shifts that first appear as a small fire erupt into an inferno of change. The same thing occurs in business cycles and business models, capitalizing upon the fuel from the zeitgeist of the time. Something happens as companies become larger, as business models and reporting structures become more complex, and as connections to the customer and to communities become more distant. The celebration of venture capital, startups and the allegiance towards the Silicon Valley model over the past few decades are symbolic of profit over purpose.

When thinking about some of the world's best-known entrepreneurs, we might envision the founders of some of the great technology companies such as Hewlett Packard (Bill Hewlett, David Packard, Mohamed Mohamed Atalla) or Apple (Steve Jobs, Steve Wozniak, Ronald Wayne) and the stories of how these companies started in garages. Many great enterprises have come from humble beginnings, and inspiration for business ideas can strike at any time, any location and any stage of life (the founder of McDonald's, Ray Kroc, was 52 when he started the global burger chain). Often the most thoughtful business models come from the most seasoned minds.

How founders tackle adversity plays a role in whether these companies become successful, and how many of them end up changing the world. The end results can be mixed, as seen with once-lauded technology companies – those that say they will do no evil and then compromise those intentions through their business models. There must be another path, one that doesn't exclude and marginalize.

The model that goes 'beyond good' is one that adjusts to changing circumstances in the world around them, including shifts in demographics, changing consumer demand and evolving points of view. Whether a business grows to be large matters not, as businesses of all sizes across all industries have an impact on the social fabric of their communities, and small businesses continue to lead that charge. The companies that are truly built to last are the ones that evolve towards the arc of the common good, not just because there are more often positive long-term financial benefits, but because it's simply the right thing to do.

In 1916, an enterprising carpenter named Ole Kirk Christiansen started a business making furniture in Billund, Denmark. His workshop experienced a fire and burned down to the ground in 1924. Like many aspiring entrepreneurs, he decided to double down and build an even larger factory. After opening the new workshop, the Great Depression impacted his sales and suppressed the successful relaunch of his furniture business. After the additional tragedies of losing his wife and experiencing two further factory fires, Ole Kirk's business was more than struggling. Within tragedy there is sometimes opportunity.

His shift from furniture building to wooden toy development prompted him to experiment more and led to the creation of a system of interlocking wooden bricks. After purchasing a plastic injection-moulding machine at the end of World War II, he and his son Godtfred patented 'Automatic Binding Bricks' in 1949. In 1953, these bricks became known as *Lego Mursten*, or 'Lego Bricks' to align with their new company name, *leg godt*, which means 'play well'.

The story of Lego has always been more than one of bricks; it has been one of change. Now Lego has answered a new call – for social change. Listening to customer feedback and seeing changing global attitudes, Lego has now fully embraced doing more for the environment and is focused on its global impact in regard to sustainable manufacturing. It has started production of plant-based polyethylene Lego sets, and plans to make the Lego product line and manufacturing process entirely sustainable by 2030.

Today, Lego toys reach 100 million children in over 140 countries. This is, as *Forbes* contributor Simon Mainwaring put it, 'a staggering opportunity to help shape and define a generation of builders, makers and dreamers that can positively impact both the culture and the planet'.[7]

The story of Lego is one of perseverance, but the lesson of Lego is so much more. It is a reflection of a company forged in traditional values, tested by fire, and one shifting to reflect the needs of a changing consumer and a changing society. It is the story of an enterprise valuing the stakeholder over that of the shareholder, a pivot that pays even more dividends in the long term, a theme you will hear throughout this book, as more companies and more industries shift towards purpose.

Longevity as the new normal

We are facing an unprecedented demographic shift, one that represents one of the most significant migrations in our human experience: longevity is becoming the new normal. Across Asia and Europe, the world's population is living much longer, with the age group of 65 and over growing the fastest.

Consider the following statistics from the United Nations Population Prospects 2019[8] and the Milken Institute, a global non-profit, non-partisan think tank:[9]

- In 2018, for the first time in history, there were more people over 65 than children under 5.
- By 2040, 1 in 4 US workers will be older than 55. The nature of work is changing.
- By 2050, 1 in 6 people in the world will be over 65 (16%), up from 1 in 11 in 2019 (9%).
- By 2050, 1 in 4 people living in Europe and North America will be aged 65 or over.

- By 2050, there will be more than twice as many older people than children under 5, and the 1.5 billion people aged 65 years or over will outnumber those aged 15 to 24 years (1.3 billion).

Over the past century, the average person has gained an extra 30 years of life and can now expect to live to 72.6 years old. But we are not merely living longer, we are also changing how we live. With vitality becoming a new norm, people are starting families later and returning to education mid-career to reskill. Not only are we seeing multiple generations working side by side, but contingent work arrangements are also becoming more common for workers that seek flexibility, fulfilment and income beyond traditional retirement age. How we enable older adults to stay productive is critical not only from an individual perspective, but also on a macro level, as they will be a key driver for job sustainability in the US and other geographies. To reap the benefits of longevity, we must rethink our approach to aging.

While aging is universal, how we age is not. Policies supporting old age should not just be focused on 'end of life', but also on how we can best the make use of the extra healthy years that we have gained. Andrew Scott, a British economist, Professor of Economics and former Deputy Dean at London Business School, frames the conversation around living longer like this: 'Longevity is about all of life and not just about the end of life. It emphasizes that society isn't just experiencing an increase in the number of old people, but that how we are aging is changing.'[10]

With declining fertility rates in many developed countries and a reduction in workforce, governments will face lower economic growth and strains on their social safety net, from healthcare to pensions and social protections, unless they focus on increasing workforce participation by women and older adults and take into consideration the influence of their policies on immigration. Home to more than half of the world's population aged 65 and over by 2030, according to the United Nations, Asia will be feeling the brunt of the impact, with people from Japan, China, South Korea, Hong Kong, Singapore and Taiwan enjoying longer lifespans than those in the US.

In extreme cases, some countries may even see a reduction in population, as is already happening with Japan; and the trend will continue. Twenty-seven countries have already experienced a population decrease of at least 1 per cent since 2010. In the next 30 years, that figure will double, with the population in China projected to shrink by 31.4 million (2.2 per cent) according to the United Nations.[11]

To get a glimpse of this future, we take a more in-depth look at demographic trends – first in Singapore, the Asian city-state with one of the highest life expectancies in the world, then Spain, whose population is growing, despite having the lowest birthrate in Europe, and then finally Japan, as it adjusts to a shrinking population and the question of immigration.

SPOTLIGHT ON SINGAPORE

There are fewer than 6 million people in Singapore as of June 2020, according to data from the government of Singapore.[12] Its declining birth rate, coupled with increased longevity, creates an *inverted* demographic pyramid, with older adults rapidly outnumbering those who are younger.

To take full advantage of increased longevity, citizens need to make sure that they stay healthy, save more and work longer. But they can't do it alone. To encourage a healthy lifestyle, the government of Singapore has partnered with Apple on a national health initiative, LumiHealth, using Apple Watch.[13] By leveraging technology and behavioural insights, the government hopes to encourage people to adopt healthier habits through personalized reminders, programmes, activity coaching and incentives.

To encourage workers to stay employed longer, the Singaporean government has also increased the retirement age – along with raising the ceiling on employment age. Under the

WorkPro scheme, companies are also incentivized to foster progressive and age-friendly workplaces and jobs. It is no wonder that Singapore enjoys a steady rise in workforce participation by older adults in the past decade, and one of the highest among OECD countries.

To empower older adults to continue to contribute to the workforce, merely raising the retirement age is insufficient, however. Through SkillsFuture initiatives, the Singapore government actively promotes lifelong learning, enabling citizens to deepen their skills and gain new ones regardless of their starting points, whether they are still in school, early- or mid-career, or older. Such initiatives to promote learning are not only advantageous to older workers seeking to change career or learn new skills, they also allow the economy to adapt to evolving technologies such as artificial intelligence, and prepare the workforce for Industry 4.0 in order to remain competitive.

For example, under the SGUnited Mid-Career Pathways Programme, SkillsFuture Singapore partnered with IBM[14] to introduce 'i.am-vitalize', a full-time skills-focused, blended-learning programme targeted at mid-career professionals, to help them combine their current expertise with digital proficiency to meet industry needs. The programme features Artificial Intelligence (AI) and Cybersecurity tracks curated by IBM Skills Academy, and IBM will also facilitate job placement opportunities to qualified candidates after programme completion.

SPOTLIGHT ON SPAIN

The demographic situation in Spain offers interesting lessons. Spain is progressively aging even as its population continues to grow. By 2050, according to the Organisation for Economic Co-Operation and Development (OECD),[15] Spain will have one of the highest percentages of older adults in the world, second only to Japan. While healthy lifestyles account for the increase in longevity, women are having fewer children, and the average age of starting a family is now 32.1. Since the early 1980s, Spain's birth rate has slowed to 2.1 babies born per woman, the very minimum to replace the current population.

One thing that is very different about Spain, however (especially when compared to Japan), is that the increased immigration rate has led to overall population growth. In the decade between 1998 and 2009, the percentage of immigrants in Spain jumped from 1.6% of its population to 12% – among the highest in Europe. As the country's policies around immigration change and the number of immigrants fluctuate, Spain will experience a decrease in its overall population growth – as well as the financial and caregiving challenges that go along with it. Compared to many other OECD countries, however, the health spending per capita in Spain is more than 15% lower than the EU average, and its social inequalities in life expectancy are also less pronounced.[16]

As in Japan and other age-friendly countries, one of the key challenges the government must tackle is the issue of loneliness. As a result, co-housing communities have sprung up in various EU countries, including Germany, Denmark, Netherlands, the UK and Spain, in order to promote healthy active aging and strengthen intergenerational bonds.[17] Age-friendly city planning, such as in Bilbao,[18] Spain, can serve as a blueprint for other cities to follow.

SPOTLIGHT ON JAPAN

Within this decade, Japan will become the world's first *ultra-aged* nation with 28% of its population aged 65 and older. Today, Japan's life expectancy is around 85 years old – 81.25 for men and 87.32 for women. While this represents positive societal norms such as healthy diets, active lifestyles and comprehensive health services focused on older populations, Japan is facing a significant challenge as its population shrinks. The total population of Japan is now expected to drop from 126 million in 2019 to 107 million in 2050, with some estimating that number going as low as 87 million by 2060.[19] For the first time since 1899, the number of babies born in Japan fell an estimated 5.9% in 2019, to under 900,000; at the same time, the country also recorded its highest number of deaths this year since the end of World War II: nearly 1.4 million.[20]

While the population is living longer, healthier lives, Japan's steadily declining fertility rate is exacerbated by its cost of living and expenses associated with raising children, as well as its historical reluctance to increase immigration levels. This demographic reality will challenge Japan's ability to maintain its standard of living as it struggles to find caregivers to look after its aging citizenry.

How Japan responds to this unprecedented population shift will be telling. These demographic pressures have been building for many decades. Some mitigating factors are being addressed through a shift in policy. The Japanese government is offering incentives for childbirth, assisting with early childcare costs, as well as reducing the number of hours that people work. Through the Specified Skills visa, immigrants can enter Japan to work in particular sectors (agriculture, nursing care, childcare, construction, manufacturing, and food and hospitality services) for a maximum period of five years. The plan to admit up to 345,000 workers under the new visa will address some of the growing labour shortages in Japan's rapidly aging society.[21] More steps will be necessary, policy changes will be required, but it is a start. Japan will likely not be alone for long as more societies age.

We are vastly unprepared for the realities of longevity. We need to develop renewed empathy towards this fastest-growing demographic and a new foundation within our social contract. As societies age, the need for caregivers and geriatricians increases. Nations are being confronted with a caregiving cliff, where the demand for care far outweighs those available to provide it. The potential support ratio, which compares the number of people of working age to those aged over 65, has been falling around the world, with Japan experiencing the lowest ratio. Adding to the challenge is the trend towards increased urbanization; more people are moving out of rural areas into metropolitan ones where the jobs are found, leaving aging parents behind and alone in their homes. In 2009, the population in the world's urban areas surpassed the proportion of people residing in rural areas; over the next few decades, the rural population is expected to plateau and eventually decline, while the population in cities and megacities worldwide will continue to grow.

Without policy changes and innovative measures, our ability to take care of the older citizens within our communities will be challenged, putting immense strain on the social services support systems. Whether a nation chooses to commoditize elder care or treat it as part of the social safety net that everyone has access to, the need to change is urgent. This is where businesses come into the picture, whether through innovating to meet the needs of the growing longevity economy, or by leveraging their life experience to complement a changing intergenerational workforce.

The future of aging should not be a story of survival – but one of living and thriving. It is through the acknowledgement of both the challenges and opportunities of aging that businesses, large and small, must begin to confront the reality of this changing tide.

Reduced social mobility

Alongside longevity, we are also experiencing decreased social mobility around the world. While technological innovation has vastly improved the wellbeing of many, and plays a crucial role in eradicating deep poverty, it has also exacerbated other forms of inequalities in our society where the 99 per cent are increasingly falling behind and the top 1 per cent are continually building upon their existing wealth.

According to The Global Social Mobility Index 2020[22] released by the World Economic Forum, very few economies have the right conditions for fostering social mobility. 'On average, across key developed and developing economies, the top 10% of earners have nearly 3.5 times the income of the bottom 40%.'[23] Unsurprisingly, the top five countries for social mobility listed in the report were all Scandinavian countries, with social democratic principles at their public policy core.

Increasingly, our chances in life are a matter of 'luck' – predetermined by the postal codes where we were born and the social class that our parents belong to, which in turn determines the level of education we will attain, the opportunities we will have access to, the line of work we will pursue, and the income we will earn. The economic costs of relocation and the lack of affordable housing in cities where the economy thrives have undermined most workers' ability to take advantage of the employment opportunities available, thereby contributing to reduced mobility across geography. With the vast majority of entrepreneurship opportunities and job growth being concentrated in a few locations (which are concurrently challenged by technological innovation and automation), our society has become more unequal and increasingly polarized. Later we will highlight how some communities are pushing back to create more localized opportunities.

The news cycle in the past few years demonstrates the social and economic impact of an unequal and fragile world driven by immobility and seclusion: distrust of institutions, erosion of the social contract, and a sense of unfairness. The weakening of the social fabric threatens to tear communities apart and spark social unrest from Asia, to Europe and the Americas. According to Oxfam's report *Time to Care*,[24] 'If everyone were to sit on their wealth piled up in $100 bills, most of humanity would be sitting on the floor. A middle-class person in a rich country would be sitting at the height of a chair. The world's two richest men would be sitting in outer space.'[25] And this is pre-Covid data, before the gap between the elite and the the society widens further.

To increase social mobility, we need to create new pathways for people in depressed economies to secure meaningful work with a living wage, as well as a bridge for those in growing cities to discover opportunities in areas that once saw decline. In the subsequent chapters of this book, we will explore how combined efforts between public and private sectors can spur viability of local economies, stimulate job growth and revive businesses throughout our communities. A fairer world is possible, and we must emulate those models that work to combat the forces of economic isolation.

In your business and your industry, how is the challenge of decreased social mobility impacting you? Whether you are in construction and manufacturing, transport or finance, your customers' ability to improve their lives both socially and financially will likely impact your business and your decisions as a leader. In turn, it will impact your life and that of your employees and team members. What is your plan to help your community reach greater equality? What is your plan to build a business that goes *Beyond Good*?

Emergence of the new self-employed and the gig economy

Businesses are no longer simply defined by brick and mortar stores with employees and benefits, including healthcare insurance, paid time off and taxes. In the last decade, we have witnessed the rise of the self-employed and contingent workers, and the trend is here to stay. According to figures from the US Census Bureau in 2016, 'more than three-fourths of US businesses may run out of someone's home and have zero employees.'[26] While ground zero for this new mode of employment is the US, the trend is also accelerating globally, as more and more work becomes contingent in nature and workers are expected to pass through waves of not just several employers, but several careers, during their extended lifetime. How will this change the way you think about the opportunities and challenges of your business?

Gig work itself is not new, as there have always been freelancers, independent contractors and temporary workers. What has changed though, is the availability of technology platforms (such as Lyft, Uber, Deliveroo, Doordash, Grubhub, Handy, TaskRabbit) and the popularity of smartphones, that bring the buyers and providers of services together. Such a model allows individuals, who are otherwise working a traditional full-time job, to find supplemental income outside their work. It's a two-sided marketplace.

While such work arrangements offer a flexibility that is not normally associated with traditional full-time work, it is not without its perils. According to a Prudential study on US gig economy workers published in 2019, on average, gig workers earn about 58 per cent less than full-time employees.[27] Posing further challenges to workers' financial wellbeing, in countries like the US that are without universal healthcare, most gig work arrangements do not provide access to traditional benefits such as insurance, paid time off and pensions, making it more difficult for gig workers to attain important financial goals, and leaving them vulnerable to financial risks. The cyclical and temporal nature of gig work also provides less income security, making it more challenging to manage day-to-day finances such as paying rent. As we have witnessed in 2020, the lack of a financial cushion can have a devastating impact on gig workers' financial wellbeing during an economic crisis. We will discuss that more fully in Chapter 7.

Today's self-employed are vastly different from those in the past – they vary in age, demographics and the types of work they do. According to recent studies from the Pew Research Center on 2018 labour-force data, '29 per cent of (Baby) Boomers, ages

65 to 72, were working or looking for work – outpacing the labour market engagement of the Silent Generation (21 per cent; born between 1928 and 1945), and the Greatest Generation (19 per cent; born between 1901 and 1927), when they were the same age.'[28] It is therefore not surprising that a third of gig-only workers are boomers, with many working post-retirement because of financial needs. This demonstrates that, as generations have progressed over the last century, more and more workers have had to seek out both more transient work and an extension of years worked compared to earlier generations.

The Freelancing in America 2019 report from Upwork further validates the growing significance of freelancing as part of the overall economy: 35 per cent of working adults participate in freelancing in some way. This mode of employment constitutes a sizable share of the economy, with income contributing to nearly 5 per cent of total US Gross Domestic Product (GDP).[29]

The implications of the changing employment model for our economy and businesses are profound. Many of these platforms not only act as a marketplace, but they also provide billing/payment services. How should incumbent financial services firms rethink their relationships with the changing needs of these customers, many of whom may not necessarily fit the traditional profile of a high-street bank customer? Of the gig-only millennials surveyed by Prudential, 'nearly half (49 per cent) say they are struggling financially, and 70 per cent say they have no access to benefits.'[30] What can policymakers do to improve the financial security of this growing demographic of workers? And how can the private sector, such as advisers and benefit solution providers, help these workers navigate their increasingly complex financial lives?

This impact also extends beyond gig workers. Take the hospitality industry as an example. The popularity of app-based ride-sharing services such as Lyft and Uber diminish the need for hired cars at hotels. Where doormen used to hail taxis for guests and collect tips in return, many are now watching ride-sharing vehicles streaming by. And instead of calling for room service, more guests are ordering food via their smartphones: Grubhub, UberEats, Deliveroo, Meituan, Ele.me, Swiggy or Gojek are just a click away.

Given the projected growth of the gig economy, this segment remains ripe for innovation – and more thoughtful dialogue. How we balance the appetite for the conveniences of the app economy and the financial wellbeing of workers must be a focus for policymakers and employers alike.

Does your company or industry leverage more transient gig workers as part of your workforce? Do you use some of these delivery services or app-based services that offer a plethora of convenience services from food and grocery delivery to odd jobs and transport? Have you thought about the long-term impact that these jobs have on these workers, your country's economy or your community? While there are positives (worker flexibility, convenient services for customers), there are many drawbacks (reduction in worker income compared to full-time work, minimal benefits such as healthcare and sick leave, environmental impacts with added food waste), and these issues must be considered as part of any company's strategic plan and its efforts to improve the opportunities for more people in its communities.

Focus on entrepreneurship

Along with the emergence of the new self-employed is the increase in entrepreneurship. According to the OECD, 'new enterprise creations (including sole proprietors) continued to increase from their crisis lows in nearly all OECD countries',[31] including Australia, France and the United Kingdom. The majority of enterprises (between 70 per cent and 95 per cent) are micro businesses[32] (eg enterprises with fewer than 10 persons employed).

For any innovation hub to prosper i.
elements: talent, funding and market re
equally distributed, opportunities are not.
States, funding for startups continues to be h
by the same three states: California, Massachu
York, raising 79 per cent of US investments in the
ter of 2020, according to the MoneyTree Report p.   y
PwC and CB Insights.[33] And the top 10 states went on t   apture
9 out of every 10 dollars invested in the second quarter of 2020,
according to the same report.[34] Perhaps, unsurprisingly, the top
global startup ecosystems, as ranked by Startup Genome in
2020, include Silicon Valley, New York City, London, Beijing,
Boston, Tel Aviv-Jerusalem and Los Angeles.[35] Not only are
these the same top seven ecosystems as those in 2019, but they
also represent a combined value of $1.5 trillion, 1.7 times the
remaining top ecosystems.[36]

Being an entrepreneur can be a lonely experience – and having
a community to lean on can make a world of difference. If you
happen to be in Silicon Valley, chances are you are familiar with
some of the hot spots in downtown Palo Alto, where techies from
all walks of life like to meet, hash out ideas, pitch and try out new
products – all over coffee (and perhaps now, all through video-
conferencing, but more on that later on as we talk about the state
of the global pandemic and inclusive business decisions).

But what if you are not in Silicon Valley? What if you are not
in New York, London or Hong Kong? How do you tap into
your local community for support? And how do we level the
playing field and redistribute the opportunities for local communities – which will not only introduce more diversity in the
startup ecosystems, but also promote economic growth and revi-
talize high streets across the world?

As Victor Hwang, Kauffman VP of Entrepreneurship,
commented in the video 'Saving Main: Betting Big on Small':
'Most people think of entrepreneurship as the lone individual

.. out there and builds a business for themselves and that ...t takes is one person with the grit to do it. But what we know now is that entrepreneurship is a community sport.'[37] It takes more than an idea – more than an individual's grit and passion. It takes the support of a community to win.

How is your company or your industry tapping into local talent outside of the big city centres? How are you promoting flexibility within the workplace and within your business model to tap into new forms of talent and new marketplaces that were previously unknown? Thanks to the power of technology and our connected world today, distance is less meaningful, and as we have seen recently, not insurmountable. Whether we own a print shop in Brussels or are a clothing manufacturer in Bangkok, we now have the ability to create value and open up opportunities to match the needs of a new age, one where we improve the lot of lives in our community.

Women empowerment

During the past decade, we have seen the emergence of the *MeToo* movement and more recognition of the need for gender equality. But progress has been painfully slow. According to the Global Gender Gap Report 2020 from the World Economic Forum (WEF), gender parity will not be attained for 99.5 years.[38] In some ways, it would appear that instead of progressing, we have taken a step backwards. The Economic Participation and Opportunity gap, for example, will now take 257 years to close[39] (compared to 202 years in the year prior). With only 55 per cent of women (aged 15–64) engaged in the labour market versus 78 per cent of men, along with over 40 per cent of the wage gap, and over 50 per cent of the income gap that have yet to be bridged,[40] it would appear that none of us will see gender parity in our lifetimes, and nor is it likely that many of our children will – despite the relentless effort to push for change.

While women have been the majority of degree-educated adults for more than a decade, it is only recently that they have reached parity with men in the degree-educated workforce, according to statistics provided by the Pew Research Center. Even though women represent half of the workforce in the US, men make up an overwhelming majority of top earners in the country, dominating highly lucrative jobs in financial services and beyond, while women overwhelmingly occupy jobs on the lower pay scale such as caregiving and hospitality. According to the Pew Research Center, 'women account for only 25 per cent of degree-educated workers in computer occupations and 15 per cent of degree-educated workers in engineering occupations.'[41]

Improving women's representation among the degree-educated labour force will have significant implications for future workers and economic parity, since advanced education translates to greater earning potential. In the long run, this could help to narrow the gender wage gap and gender leadership gap, with the latter being highlighted by the general lack of women among the executive ranks of S&P 500 companies. As of mid-September 2020, women hold only 32 CEO positions (6.4 per cent) at S&P 500 companies, according to Catalyst.org.[42] At the top 25 highest-valued public companies identified by *The New York Times*, there are no women.[43]

Unfortunately, some of the progress that has been made in years past might be wiped out owing to the economic downturn. According to the Bureau of Labor Statistics, for instance, four times more women than men dropped out of the labour force in the US in September 2020.[44] As families are struggling to balance work duties and childcare, women are increasingly bearing the brunt of the crisis.

We simply cannot build an inclusive society and truly inclusive business models until we change the status quo. While women are at the core of *Beyond Good*, we must push for equal recognition as well. Beyond stewardship, women are notably missing in mass media publications. Consider the following:

- In the *Forbes* list of top 100 innovators in 2019, there was only one woman – out of 100 names.
- In the *Harvard Business Review* list of top 100 CEOs in 2019, only 4 women made the list, out of 100 names, compared to 3 in the previous year.
- For the 2019 *Time* magazine 'Person of the Year', Greta Thunberg became the 5th woman to take the honour, in the magazine's 90-year history.

The case for women empowerment is even more compelling if we focus on the impact from frontier technologies. Faced with new pressures from automation, McKinsey Global predicts that between 40 million to 160 million women (7 to 24 per cent of all women in the workforce today) may need to transition across jobs and skill sets by 2030 to remain employed.[45]

We need new creative solutions to help women adapt and thrive in the new era – and such efforts need to come from both private and public sectors. On one hand, they need to be skilled and tech savvy to meet the demands of the new jobs created; on the other, they need to be flexible and mobile enough – with access to the right networks – to pursue these new opportunities.

If women are not able to make the transition from lower-paying jobs that are threatened by automation – into higher-paying roles, the current gender pay gap between men and women might worsen. More must be done to retrain and equip women with new skill sets – whether they are part of the existing workforce or seeking to return to work from extended leave via returnship programmes.

But improving educated women's representation in the work-force does not, and cannot, happen in a vacuum. To have sustaining positive impact, diversity is only the beginning – while inclusion represents the other side of the same coin. To attract and retain diverse staff, companies must maintain a welcoming environment that allows different voices to be heard, and different personalities to thrive. This also requires family-friendly policies that support flexible work arrangements, since women typically act as the primary caregiver for their children and aging parents.

At present, the United States is the only industrialized nation in the world that does not offer paid parental leave. Changing such a policy will go a long way in enabling higher women workforce participation and normalizing men's role in caregiving, putting women one step closer to parity. Without intentional and substantial changes, it will take close to a century to close the overall global gender gap, and many more years to close the Economic Participation and Opportunity gap as mentioned earlier – a timeline that is simply unacceptable.

We believe that every voice in every community matters, and that it is up to all of us to make sure the needs of each one is heard. In what ways is your business improving the lives of women in your community? How is your industry changing the dynamic for women in the workplace? From formal mentoring programmes to supportive infrastructure and training to recognize both bias and harassment, the presence of women in both the workplace and in the development of the next generation of business leaders will be a significant factor in all markets. How are you going to be part of this significant shift, one where more women are making key decisions at all levels? Choose your path wisely, or risk losing the future to other businesses that are far more inclusive.

We must add diversity (gender, age, ethnicity, language, etc) to all teams that want to move the needle, or we will continue to talk and not do enough. HEIDI CULBERTSON, CEO AND FOUNDER OF MARVEE

Economic, social and cultural implications

Along with life and death, change is one of the pure certainties in life. The condition of our life transforms over time as our societies, community and circumstances change. Given how we have shifted our approach to learning, working and living, it is no longer meaningful to segment our lives by biological age, nor is it logical to assume we all follow the traditional trajectory of a three-stage life of education, career and retirement. Education can occur throughout our professional life, as working longer requires us to stay current with our skill sets. Our career will be a series of applications of our learning and experiences, with more options being added every year. Retirement will also take on a new meaning as more people volunteer or work part-time post full-time employment, and as we age longer.

How will companies and communities react to this new landscape? Business models should reflect changes in our culture to best serve the needs of over 7.5 billion people. At the centre of these changes is economic opportunity and the ability for society to take care of our basic needs – food, water, shelter – as well as the new requirements of an increasingly digital age driving new forms of inequality. How key industries evolve – especially financial services (as we will see in the coming chapters) – will be an important factor in how many of us live comfortable, fulfilling lives.

While each of our ecosystems is unique and each of our communities has its distinctive characteristics, we have more in common than we are commonly led to believe. We are all one species. We all share the same biology, the same humanity. As technology continues to make the world smaller and more connected, we have a chance to build a more inclusive society – one where we meet more than our basic needs.

CHAPTER TWO

Foundations of inclusion

*We all should know that diversity makes for a rich tapestry,
and we must understand that all the threads of the tapestry are
equal in value no matter their colour; equal in importance no
matter their texture.*[1] MAYA ANGELOU

Starting with the basics

To develop the principles of *Beyond Good* – how businesses
become better stewards for all stakeholders – we must first
explore how inclusive business practices can improve the condition of communities. We also look at what challenges are
emerging – some of which we identified in the last chapter – and
which societal issues are improving. We have to start with some
foundational questions and then work towards definitions.
What factors of inequality act to impede more focus on the

common good? How do we build truly inclusive communities, ones that embrace proven solutions for very diverse needs, so that we don't repeat mistakes from the past? What are some solutions that are working today?

Inclusion itself is a loaded word, one that elicits division as it seeks to embrace. We've established the changing nature of work, the rise of entrepreneurship, the aging of societies, and the challenges to achieving gender diversity and broader inclusion among the shifting tides. How can we possibly include everyone in the spoils of human endeavour, maximizing every output through every input? How can the pie of opportunity be split more fairly into 7.5 billion pieces? Yet this is what we must strive to achieve. Business leaders face challenges all the time, but building inclusive business practices is different. From Beijing to Minsk, from Chicago to Calcutta, in our roles in construction, software development, medicine or financial services, it is always possible to improve the impact of the externalities of your business by viewing things through a broader lens. While that may not help you fix your payroll system, inclusive models may help your revenue, as you choose to do well by doing good. We will dive much more into that in later chapters.

In today's global political climate, societies too often frame the question of more inclusive business practices as a set of values of the individual versus those of one's community. This is also associated with political leanings towards opposing narratives. In reality, it is a question of empathy driving deeper community awareness. If you have to give up something to benefit others – such as lowering the cost of a good you supply to certain markets where people have lower incomes – why does it feel like something was lost? While communities also face these trade-offs – in exchange for paying taxes, you receive a certain level of healthcare or financial safety, emergency services or government protections – there remains a growing divide between rich and poor, between gender, race and our perceived differences. Businesses must change their perception of responsibility to their community. Purpose must be redefined in a more communal way.

As we view the basic human needs of food, water and shelter, we must focus on expanding beyond subsistence. While inclusion and inclusiveness are different concepts from diversity, we need to ensure no one – no group – is left behind (or systematically favoured above another). This includes the communities, businesses and organizations that we belong to and those we aspire to. This encompasses the opportunities we have and the ability to create better options for others. Inclusion surrounds almost every aspect of our lives, starting at the very beginning at our birth, before bias and blinders take form, and before barriers transform aspiration into an impossible dream.

Luck of the draw

Think about where you were born – the physical locations of your childhood. Visualize your earliest memories of your parents, any siblings, the family members you knew growing up. You might imagine the house you lived in, the neighbourhood, the toys you played with, the scents of the kitchen, those early hobbies or travels, those memories imprinted in your mind. In thinking about these earliest experiences, do you remember what you worried about? What were your greatest concerns?

Each generation has challenges that they become aware of as they age – the politics and turbulence of events that impact their family, the level of comfort or struggle brought on by economic conditions, the amount they moved around or were stable, their perception of their place in the class or caste of their community. Try to recall ways you wished you could change the world – things that you felt could impact your future or that of your family. The way we each look at the problems of the world is dependent on our unique personal perspectives and our individual experiences growing up.

This is one of the most explicit realities in life: where we were born has one of the most significant impacts on what we can potentially achieve. How we think about pretty much everything stems from these formative years. How we are rooted opens up our mind as well as feeds our limitations. It defines the set of choices we start our life with, and as we age, how our families adapt. Our upbringing impacts location-driven opportunities requiring greater physical mobility as well as a degree of class mobility that creates different paths ahead of us. Our very lives are rooted in this upbringing. The businesses we lead are heavily influenced by this, as well. We can't feel what we don't see.

The path towards broader inclusion – especially financially driven inclusion – starts with acknowledgement of structural impediments within our personal lives, our communities and our cultures. As we personally integrate ourselves into our communities over our lifetime and touch other lives through our actions, how we choose to help and influence others also has an impact. As we establish our own path, we must leverage the realities of the luck (or hindrance) of where we were born and create opportunities for others. This is how generations scale ladders and how our networks open up avenues.

The role of money

If the luck of where we were born is a central component in securing life's basic needs, how money (or the lack thereof) influences the quality of our lives is very critical. The role of money changes your assumptions, influences you and impacts how your life evolves. Going back to earlier, what did you worry about when growing up? According to an ongoing global study by the World Economic Forum,[2] the top ten most concerning world issues that worry younger people around the globe today include the following:

- climate change (48.8%);
- conflict and wars (38.9%);
- income inequality (30.8%);
- poverty (29.2%);
- religious conflicts (23.9%);
- government transparency/corruption (22.7%);
- food and water security (18.2%);
- lack of education (15.9%);
- safety, security and personal wellbeing (14.1%);
- lack of economic opportunity and employment (12.1%).

At the heart of the majority of these concerns is money. Our worries are constructed around the lack of money and the associated lack of opportunity, as well as our ability to control our life's trajectory. Income inequality, poverty, access to food and water, education, safe and secure places to live, opportunity and employment – all of these have to do with money.

Think about your own relationship with money, how you first learned about what it was and what it meant. Think about what money meant to you and your family and the opportunities you had and those that weren't part of your life choices. It all ties back to where you were born and your development of attitudes, limitations and aspirations around the truly simple concept of value exchange.

Contrast this with people who live without much money at all. The World Bank estimates that there are 734 million people[3] living on less than $1.90 a day. While the percentage of people globally who live in extreme poverty has come down significantly in the last 25 years, nearly 10 per cent of the 7.5 billion on this planet struggle to meet their very basic needs.

As humanity evolved, we went from the drive to fulfil basic needs to create a vast world teeming with more complex activities – one that wasn't set up well to evenly meet the expanding needs and wants of 7.5 billion people. Despite breakthroughs in technology that have improved our lives, we have created more complex and dire problems such as climate change that not only concern our younger generations, but should also provide perspective on how the thinking of business leaders must evolve. We live in a very connected world, where every business, every industry is interconnected and where personal and professional choices matter.

Our perspectives shift constantly, even as our roots try to keep us grounded. How have we collectively evolved to meet the problems of the world? While our tools and institutions have evolved – many solutions have become digital now (and this took less than a century of modernization) – how much have we really evolved to meet our most basic needs across the full spectrum of humanity? Sometimes, when we try to think about the big problems that the world faces, we take these basic building blocks for granted. We may also miss the forest for the trees when it comes to understanding how the world around us is changing, and how much our personal actions and leadership decisions are part of that transformation, especially how uneven economic opportunity is for so many.

The state of inequality

While global extreme poverty is being greatly reduced and the wealth inequality between countries has fallen, income and wealth inequality within countries has been steadily rising. This is nowhere more apparent than in the United States, where the top 1 per cent holds 42.5 per cent of national wealth, according to data from the OECD.[4] Meanwhile, the household income for the top 1 per cent in the UK has almost tripled in the past four decades, while that of the lowest-earning households has barely risen.[5] Both the US and the UK experienced increases in the shares of the top 5 per cent and top 1 per cent respectively, and declines in the shares of the bottom 60 per cent and 40 per cent respectively between 2010 and 2016.

Between 1990 and 2020, 'US billionaire wealth soared 1,130 per cent in 2020 dollars, an increase more than 200 times greater than the 5.37 per cent growth of US median wealth over this same period.'[6] 'In no other industrial nation does the richest 1 per cent own more than 28 per cent of their country's wealth.'[7]

Globally, the picture is just as dire. According to Credit Suisse Global Wealth Report 2019, 'While more than half of all adults worldwide have a net worth below $10,000, nearly 1 per cent of adults are millionaires who collectively own 44 per cent of global wealth.'[8] While the 'bottom half of adults accounts for less than 1 per cent of total global wealth in mid-2019, the top 10 per cent of adults possess 82 per cent of global wealth.'[9]

Financial inequality impacts our ability to create wealth, achieve greater wage independence and build a sense of security. The role of opportunity around wealth and money also impacts populations and demographics very differently. Much of this is created by gender and racial disparities, from care-giving demands to pay gaps, which we examine in later chapters. There is a drastic imbalance in unpaid household and care work that women perform. Culturally, historically and geographically, women are *expected* to be the primary caregiver of the family; the United Nations has estimated that 'women do 2.6 times the amount of unpaid care and domestic work that men do.'[10]

Many women pause their career or choose jobs with more flexible work arrangements that will allow them time away. In the US, for example, 60 per cent of the nation's 40 million caregivers are women. In order to care for their parents or loved ones, many caregivers take an average of 12 years break from their careers. This not only creates barriers to career advancement and reduces savings for women, it can also result in reduced future earning power and economic security.

As Melinda Gates noted in a recent interview: 'On average, the time women spend performing unpaid labour amounts to seven more years than men. That's the time it takes to complete a bachelor's and master's degree.'[11]

Globally, 42 per cent of women of working age are outside the paid labour force owing to such unpaid caregiving work, and the monetary value of unpaid caregiving work for women aged 15 and above is at least $10.8 trillion according to Oxfam.[12] Imagine the positive impact on the economic power of women and the economies that they support if we were to redistribute the caregiving burden more fairly within the households, and reduce the burden on women through better access to technologies and support infrastructure. Imagine what policy changes could be brought about if women had more equal representation in politics. A fairer world – a more equal society – would be possible.

How does your business take into account the types of gender discrepancies that impact both your employees and your customers? How can you ensure that the needs of women are an integral part of your decision making? As technology across industries moves us more towards tools and algorithms and automation, how do we ensure that new forms of bias do not increase the opportunity gap across genders?

A tale of two economies

When we think of broadening opportunities to improve monetary inclusion – beyond gender and towards geography – we can look to the developing economies throughout Africa and Southeast Asia. Compared to much of the West, the financial infrastructure of the developing world was originally designed for the needs of the very wealthy, as most of the population fell outside the traditional financial systems. For much of the past century, there has been a lack of legacy banking infrastructure to contend with – payments, card networks, credit systems – often because it has been deemed unnecessary. Financial services innovation has been uneven in its attempts to meet basic financial needs.

Even in more developed economies such as the US, the UK and much of Europe, there remain pockets of the population that are not well served by today's banking infrastructure. Concerns are growing that people are increasingly being left behind in the new digital era, with financial services retreating behind the glass screens of mobile phones and the black boxes of algorithms. While the West strives for optimization, many geographies are still working on broadening access. There is still much work to do as the industry contends with both the changing demographics of those they serve and the changing economic conditions of these communities. It is likely that this is already impacting on your business.

How can financial services better enable society to better fulfil basic needs? How can the industry move beyond basic needs to helping everyone thrive? Having a bank account is just the beginning. Merely having a relationship with a financial institution, or a means to store and move money, does not automatically alleviate poverty or reduce inequality – identifying what consumers need and what they can do with this access to banking services is where the real impact is. While we can measure success by the reduction of the unbanked population, are we measuring what truly matters?

As we will discuss more fully in the next few chapters, there remain 1.7 billion adults worldwide that are unbanked – without any access to the formal financial services system. This reflects a seven-percentage-point increase since 2014,[13] mostly propelled by a new generation of financial services such as M-Pesa and Alipay, accessed via mobile phones. The advent of mobile phones, mobile money and mobile credit systems has enabled many of these economies to leapfrog the West in terms of efforts to bring more people into the traditional economic system. But access alone isn't enough. What about improving people's lives and long-term financial security?

The industry certainly extracts a lot of value from communities in terms of profit, but what is it giving back in return? Banks would benefit more in the longer term by expanding their influence and role in delivering even the most basic needs to their entire community. Are we looking at the way in which banks can improve the financial health and success of the communities they serve? Perhaps that's what banks should focus on providing to all customers across every community – financial health. But few banks are looking at this at all. For now, short-term thinking about the value exchanged between bank customers and banks themselves is leaving too many people behind in the process.

A deeper dive is required to learn what it means to broaden financial inclusion, what grounds have been gained from digital innovation, and who is left behind. This provides a better understanding of what it would take to broaden access and create a more inclusive ecosystem. As we develop business models that go *Beyond Good*, we must consider how financial inequalities can be alleviated in any form. How can more businesses and industries be involved in meeting our very basic needs, and how many more business models can be tuned to optimize our lives? Later, when we discuss embedded finance, there may be a few ideas that can apply to your industry as the function of banking disappears and the value of it reemerges.

Meeting basic needs

For many of us – especially in Western Europe and the US – our basic needs are being met. But hunger is slowly on the rise again after decades of slow decline. It is estimated that 'nearly 690 million people are hungry, or 8.9 per cent of the world population – up by 10 million people in one year and by nearly 60 million in five years', based on figures from the report 'The State of Food Security and Nutrition in the World' (SOFI).[14] Nearly 1 in 10 people in the world were exposed to severe levels of food insecurity in 2019. In all, moderate or severe food insecurity affects an estimated 25.9 per cent of the world population – about 2 billion people, with women being more likely than men to face moderate or severe food insecurity, according to the FAO.[15] The pandemic and resulting economic downturn are expected to deteriorate the situation further, affecting people from all walks of life, including 88 million people in North America and Europe.[16]

Some of the contributors to the worsening trend include climate change, conflict and uneven economic conditions and opportunities. Perhaps unsurprisingly, high commodity-dependent countries (eg those in South America) are more susceptible to economic shocks triggered by commodity price swings, which in turn impacts access to basic needs such as food and healthcare services. Sluggish economics can also lead to unemployment, loss of income and reduction in consumer purchasing power.

Are economic growth and access to financial services the solution to food insecurity? Will robust growth automatically translate into a reduction in poverty and inequality? As it turns out, the reality is more nuanced. Our most basic human needs aren't being fulfilled consistently, and while many areas of our economy have vastly improved, progress towards closing the gaps is very uneven. As business leaders, we must become more aware of the injustices in the communities that our businesses serve. What can you do through your role in your industry to make systematic differences?

Access to water as a human right

In addition to affordable food and shelter, water is also increasingly becoming a factor in inequality. In 2010, the UN General Assembly explicitly recognized the human right to water and sanitation. According to figures from the World Health Organization and UNICEF:[17]

- One in three people or 2.2 billion people around the world lack safe drinking water.
- Over half of the global population or 4.2 billion people lack safe sanitation.
- Two out of five people or 3 billion people around the world lack basic hand-washing facilities at home; almost half of the schools in the world do not have hand-washing facilities with soap and water available to students.

And while substantial gains have been made, access is still far from equal, especially for those living in rural areas and those that are poor. Contaminated water and inadequate sanitation expose the population to preventable diseases, and also disproportionately affect women and young girls across low-income countries, since they bear the primary responsibilities for collecting clean water, standing in line for hours or walking long distances in search of water. Consider the following: '207 million people spent over 30 minutes per round trip to collect water from an improved source.'[18]

Improving access to important resources can improve health and save time – time that could be spent pursuing education and work opportunities that can help break the cycle of poverty. Economically, water scarcity will make it increasingly harder for low-income nations to thrive. In many cases, this is already happening.

SPOTLIGHT ON INDIA

Currently in second place with 1.37 billion people, India is projected to surpass China in around 2027[19] to become the most populous country in the world. Unfortunately, such a trajectory is not without serious implications. Apart from increasing demand from the growing population and lack of infrastructure to support urban growth, India faces additional challenges from climate change, which is causing sea levels to rise and Himalayan glaciers to melt more rapidly.

In between droughts and floods, an estimated 820 million people in India will experience water scarcity. As of 2014, no major city in India has been able to supply water consistently around the clock to its entire urban population.[20]

According to the latest report by NITI Aayog (National Institution for Transforming India):

- 82 per cent of rural households in India do not have individual piped water supply, and 163 million live without access to clean water close to their homes.

- 70 per cent of India's surface water is contaminated.

If India maintains the status quo, its water demand will 'exceed supply by a factor of two by 2030, with severe water scarcity on the horizon for millions.' And 6 per cent of its GDP will be lost by 2050 as a result of the water crisis.[21]

If the situation sounds dire, it is. Adding to the challenge is the massive need stemming from agriculture, which uses more than 80 per cent of the water, making it the single largest drain on the nation's water supplies.

The gap between where we are – and where we need to be – is both sad and troubling. Water management will be a crucial task, not just for India, but for nations around the world in this coming decade.

SPOTLIGHT ON SAN FRANCISCO

While much of the US has recovered after the Great Recession of 2008, the economic recovery has been uneven. Many of the opportunities generated remain concentrated in a handful of geographies. As mentioned in Chapter 1, while talent is equally distributed, opportunity is not. Funding for startups within the US continues to be heavily dominated by the same three states: California, Massachusetts and New York, raising 79 per cent of US investments in the second quarter of 2020.[22]

As the global economy continues its journey in the digital era, where tech-heavy industries play an outsized role in creating jobs and economic growth, we can imagine a widening divide between a handful of coastal innovation centres and the rest of the country. 'Rather than growing together, the nation's regions, metropolitan areas and towns have been growing apart.'[23]

This divergence between regions not only creates an imbalance in job creation, wages, investment, economic vitality and access to opportunities, it impacts access to some of our most basic needs: food and affordable housing within fast-growing cities. Meanwhile, the rest of the United States, including the *flyover states* between the coasts, suffer from talent loss along with economic and population decline.

With a population nearing 40 million, a $3 trillion economy and record low unemployment (assessed pre-pandemic), the Golden State is home to some of the world's leading and most valuable technology companies, including Apple, Facebook, Google, Oracle and Salesforce. Its median household income has grown about 17 per cent since 2011,[24] far outpacing the national average. On paper, its economic growth – and its potential – is astonishing.

Yet, the state also has sky-high housing costs and suffers from a high homelessness rate (ranking #5 in the country): of the half million who are homeless in the US, one in four lives in California. A United Nations representative, Leilani Farha, once compared an Oakland encampment to slums in Delhi, noting that 'neither has access to running water.'[25] That this dichotomy of conditions can exist in large cities like San Francisco and the surrounding Bay Area is not a new reality, but it is something that can be solved.

While there is not one single cause for homelessness, economic hardship is an often-cited reason. This can be due to the loss of a job or medical shock; or people can simply be unable to make ends meet owing to the high cost of living. Perhaps, not surprisingly, one in eight Californians struggle with food insecurity according to the California Association of Food Banks, even though the state is also the largest producer of fruit and vegetables within the United States. Post-pandemic (which we discuss later), this has become worse.

Gender and race disparity

More people in society are vulnerable to the disruption of basic needs than we likely know, and some groups are impacted more disproportionately than others. As we moved away from hunter-gatherer to agricultural societies and then to our complex modern-day civilization, the gender differences continued to evolve. When we look at inequality in terms of access to basic needs, there is a great deal of variability from one region to the next, from one social class to another. But there are also another two identities that play key roles when it comes to equality: our gender and our race.

A study conducted by New America on balancing work and care finds that 'One in four women in America (26 per cent) say that in the last year or two caregiving demands have had a negative impact on their ability to keep a job or advance in the workplace.'[26] But that number tells only half the story. In breaking down the data set further, the realities of race become much clearer. According to the report, '40 per cent of Asian women in America and 39 per cent of Latinas said that their jobs or careers were disrupted by caregiving demands.' As it turns out, Latinas, Asian American and Pacific Islander women are much more likely to report that their careers are disrupted by caregiving demands.

It will also be worth noting that the United States is the only developed country without paid parental leave, making attaining a work and life balance more daunting. We will be exploring this topic in more depth in later chapters.

What could be causing such discrepancies? Could it be cultural perceptions of what responsibilities a mother is supposed to bear? Or the presence of extended family and community to support caregiving duties, as suggested by Dawn Marie Dow, author of *Mothering While Black: Boundaries and burdens of middle-class parenthood?*[27]

As mentioned earlier in the chapter, the expectation that women should bear the brunt of unpaid domestic work is unfortunately also not limited to US mothers. According to the United Nations, women do 2.6 times the unpaid care and domestic work that men do.[28] And such unequal distribution of unpaid work disempowers individual women and hurts economies. Globally, a two-hour increase in women's unpaid care work is correlated with a ten-percentage-point decrease in women's labour-force participation.[29]

In the days of modern parenthood where dual-income families are prevalent – especially in developed economies – what would parents need in order to help them better balance the competing demands of paid employment and raising children? What policies could help bring more inclusion to our workplace? What would companies deploying the principles of *Beyond Good* do to alleviate some of this exclusion?

Extending beyond gender, vast racial inequality exists between different demographics of society. Disparities owing to factors such as education, housing and employment have diminished the prospects for many Black and Hispanic families in the US, leading to lower lifetime income and reduced intergenerational wealth, leaving many households more vulnerable to economic hardships.

According to Citigroup, 'the median amount of housing wealth for a Black family was $124,000, while the median amount for white families was $200,000, Hispanic households $158,000.'[30] Meanwhile, the gap between white and Black familial income is a multiple of eight.[31]

Given that there are countless race and gender discrepancies that impact both the quality of life and inequality of our communities, how can your business or industry work to include more people in the benefit of what you produce? How is technology enabling better assessments and countermovement towards any unintended bias based on the type of services you offer? When we acknowledge the different lives we lead compared to others in our community, especially in regard to race and gender, we start to realize how unequal society has become, and how we may unknowingly be contributing to some of its challenges.

Inclusive entrepreneurship

Broad societal inclusion can only be realized when the monetary inequalities of our communities are truly addressed. Money drives opportunities, and opportunities start to collect momentum and create positive impact across generations – much like the business flywheel from *Good to Great*. As we are faced with unprecedented challenges in our society today, from the climate crisis to rising social and economic inequality, we need new forms of thoughtful business foundation. Facilitating entrepreneurship has become one way to reduce unemployment, increase labour market participation and create wealth.

Unfortunately, while talent is equally distributed, opportunities are not. Populations such as women, youth, the unemployed and immigrants are under-represented when it comes to business creation in the EU, according to OECD's report on 'The Missing Entrepreneurs':[32]

- Women are almost half as likely as men to be involved in starting a new business, they tend to operate different types of businesses from men, and access to funding and networks continues to be a challenge.

- The 50-plus are the largest group of self-employed people in the EU. While entrepreneurship holds the promise of extending a productive working life and reducing pressure on social safety nets, age bias and tensions between generations can hinder the effort.
- For the past two decades, immigrants have become a rapidly growing group of entrepreneurs, doubling from 1.9 million in 2002 to 3.6 million in 2018. To maximize the potential, tailored programmes to provide a support network are crucial.
- While nearly half of young people express an interest in entrepreneurship, less than 5% of youth in the EU (7.4% in OECD countries) were actively trying to start a business between 2014 and 2018; business survival rate remains low.

Inclusive entrepreneurship is an integral part of inclusive growth; we need an economy that works for more people. From creating supportive networks to improving access to capital, we must be more intentional in improving the diversity and inclusivity of our entrepreneur ecosystem. This will help more businesses focus on ways to help meet basic needs in their own communities. As policies develop, we must acknowledge the heterogeneity of our population and the diverse needs of the ecosystem, beyond gender, age and ethnicity.

The purpose of a company shapes the mark it makes. The only way to build a sustainable, profitable business is to have a purpose that creates a world people want to be in. JUSTIN BOOGAARD, CO-FOUNDER AT GOGOGRANDPARENT

Levelling the playing field

We are still not on a level playing field. We need to inoculate more industries – especially financial services – with a new kind of global mission to combat the diseases associated with inequality:

poverty, hunger, disease, conflicts. Many industries have ways to help better deliver our basic needs – food, water, shelter and more – but helping us gain access to savings, payments, investments, capital, credit and the security that these build over generations is primarily catered for by one industry.

We need to move beyond the basics. Providing access to financial services is one step – helping optimize money for more people is an evolutionary component of what is truly needed (as we will detail more fully throughout the rest of the book). Inequality is a human-created problem that can be solved. And so many positive outcomes arise as we inch towards global financial inclusion and the optimization of financial opportunity.

As we look at the industry today, one thing is very clear: the banking system is changing, very rapidly. The financial services model is evolving, and banks and institutions that make up the financial services ecosystem can't remain fixated on the business model of the past. The industry should fully appreciate that it has a social contract with the communities it serves, and should play an important role in the formation of equality. Adam Smith's invisible hand isn't going to help us reach global financial inclusion – but the changes happening to the industry will.

So, what do we have to do to create a more inclusive banking system? We should focus on digitizing and optimizing identity and access to the financial system. We must increase the digitization of government payments and agricultural payments, the optimization of person to person (P2P) and person to business (P2B) payments, and continue the march of low-cost remittance. We need to put a greater focus on building up savings and investment, and optimizing spending and credit to match those innovations in other geographies – efforts to create systematic financial health and long-term financial security to help alleviate the impacts of extreme poverty.

How does your industry or your business come into play? How does your work intersect with this next iteration of the financial services business model and our call to do more for our communities? The function of money, the reason that banking exists, is to facilitate the transfer of value between one entity and another. Unfortunately, this exchange is not always equal. But you can help make the friction and cost of banking services become a smaller burden on our communities by examining ways to reduce its impact on your cash flow, and create new ways for the utility of banking to become part of your business value.

Tech-enabled alternative banking services can now provide access to credit, help build savings, connect to a broader marketplace of products and services, and help optimize your customers' spending habits, enabling them to improve their financial health. We must encourage new forms of innovation based on open data, open banking and opportunities to connect financial and non-financial value systems through embedded finance and beyond, as the function of banking recedes into the background. In many markets, this has already started, as the past decade has been the most revolutionary period in financial services' history.

CHAPTER THREE

Forces of disruption

No pessimist ever discovered the secrets of the stars, or sailed to an uncharted land, or opened a new heaven to the human spirit.[1] HELEN KELLER

The dawn of purpose

Every single day, billions of people around the globe exchange their time and productivity for income to take care of their needs and those of their families. People are stitched together by economic systems, which are supported by technology and traditions, weaving a complex fabric to meet their needs through their collective actions. What connects us in these interchanges across firms, factories and fields? Money. As monetary transfers between our varied forms of work and compensation take place, our efforts help fulfil basic needs – and for a smaller number of people – bring an inordinate level of remuneration in comparison. This is why helping people obtain, optimize and sustain their money is critically important.

Therein lies the opportunity to build on the principles of *Beyond Good* towards models that create possibilities to deliver more than our basic needs. Previously, we explored the gravity surrounding access to food, water and shelter, as well as potential headwinds in meeting necessities: shifts in demographics, social mobility, the changing nature of work, race and gender disparity, all culminating in the complex nature of inequality. As we look towards working solutions – and industries – that mitigate the impact of societal negatives and improve the common good, where is the best place to start?

To fulfil more than just basic needs – to help more people within our communities truly thrive – we will require a more responsive financial services ecosystem. Banking service providers (and all the businesses that rely upon them) must be geared towards serving the needs of everyone, not just the segments of our population that appear profitable in the short term. Financial products and services often mirror basic needs: payments and monetary transfers help us exchange labour for goods; savings and current accounts enable us to manage and store our wages; investments and insurance help us protect wealth and financial legacies. Yet, the reality is that these financial needs are met as unevenly as our basic needs. We are then as equal as the mirror that we choose to hold. Most businesses don't think this way, but maybe more should.

As we noted in Chapter 2, there remain nearly 1.7 billion people that are unbanked[2] and more that are vastly *underbanked*. Most of the global population are not seeing their finances optimized, let alone developing the financial underpinnings to improve the conditions of subsequent generations. The financial services industry holds the key to the majority of these gaps. It acts as a catalyst for access and optimization of capital while simultaneously holding the capacity to address more accountability for impact on our communities. Simply put, they are the gatekeepers to unlocking the *value* of money.

Whether banking executives acknowledge it or not, the industry also has the greatest impact on economic inclusion. But inclusion alone cannot be the end goal when we are unable to provide enough food, water and housing for everyone – when only some of us thrive while others do not. What are the primary forces of disruption that can level the playing field that we find ourselves on today? Part of it will come from optimizing opportunities around capital, compensation and the creation of wealth. We must look beyond existing business models for solutions and seek to understand real impact – from the public and private sectors, policymaking and from industries beyond banking. This remains the challenge – for banking and nearly every industry – in our quest to create a model that goes *Beyond Good.*

Serving the unbanked and underbanked

Having access to employment, being able to exchange goods and services, creating and leveraging savings over time – along with the ability to move money, store money, access credit and invest – these are some of the growing economic expectations within a modern society. These functions should also be a basic human right, given the critical role of money. Access to banking services – alongside our ability to control decisions regarding health, mobility and the monetization of our personal data and identity – have quickly become as much of a necessity in modern society as having a mobile phone.

Just as we should have an expectation of safe and sustainable communities, we must continue our efforts to achieve global financial inclusion. Our collective goal should be to ensure that everyone has *access* to basic banking services – whether they are performed at a bank or not – and that there are ways to *optimize* the value of money in our lives. Things have improved on this front. In just the past six years, the percentage of banked adults globally has gradually increased: from 51 per cent in 2011 to 62 per cent in 2014, and 69 per cent in 2017, with a total of 1.2 billion people worldwide having gained access to bank and mobile-money accounts.[3]

While this is tremendous progress, there are still 1.7 billion people unbanked – about 22 per cent of the global population, half of whom are concentrated in seven nations – China, India, Pakistan, Indonesia, Nigeria, Mexico and Bangladesh. Which means we still have much more work to do. Based on World Bank data, 62 per cent of the unbanked have not attained a primary education. They tend to be twice as likely to be living in the poorest households within their given countries. Three in 10 of those unbanked are between the ages of 15 and 24 and 47 per cent are unemployed. There is also a distinct gender gap: women are more likely to lack access to the formal financial system.

According to the same World Bank study,[4] the most commonly cited barriers to opening a bank account include:

- not having enough money (60%);
- not feeling the need for an account (37%);
- others in family have an account (35%);
- bank is too far away (24%);
- not having proper documentation to open an account (21%);
- lack of trust in the banking system (18%).

While not everyone feels they need a bank account – or some feel they lack the ability to obtain one – most people need a way to make payments for basic goods and services. This is why there is so much focus on getting more people access to transactional banking services. The one area banks themselves need to continue to focus on is trust, and that can be enhanced by helping people optimize their financial lives. This is easier said than done, as most of the global population remains vastly underbanked.

From access to optimization

Access to financial services is a critical component towards ensuring that we meet the growing needs of our diverse communities. Beyond banking's role in providing basic necessities – food, water, shelter – we also need the ability to optimize financial services, the building blocks of prosperity. Too many people are still unbanked or underbanked, and the challenges in our communities are growing as our societies age, as the nature and compensation for work shifts, and as inequalities in income and opportunity for women and under-represented demographics translate into barriers to success.

This story of financial inclusion can also take different turns depending on where you live, and one thing remains universal – access, the traditional way of measuring financial inclusion, is not enough. Having access to financial services is merely the beginning of a long journey fraught with additional challenges. These challenges are demonstrated in the following examples:

- Enabled by the surge in popularity of FinTech (financial technology startups) solutions in **Kenya,** many people who were otherwise unbanked have been able to get access to banking services including credit through FinTech apps such as M-Pesa. A 2019 survey[5] indicated that 'formal financial inclusion had increased from 27 per cent of Kenya's population in 2006 to 83 per cent.' But while lending is easy, responsible lending is much harder. Credit can help entrepreneurs start a small business, but it can also increase consumer debt when consumers end up relying on debt. Case in point: 'In Kenya, at least one out of every five borrowers struggles to repay their loan.'[6]
- **India** has made massive strides towards improving financial inclusion. As of 2017, almost 80 per cent of adult Indians had bank accounts, according to the Global Findex Database (GFD);[7] that is up from 40 per cent in 2011. However, not all gains are

equally distributed. The country currently ranks 149th out of 153 in terms of Economic Participation and Opportunity in the 2020 World Economic Forum Global Equality Index.[8] With much of the focus on access to credit, other aspects of financial services such as savings and microinsurance, along with access to income generation, cannot be ignored, in order to move the needle on equality and truly transform society across geography and gender.

- On the surface, the state of financial inclusion in the **United States** is improving as well – with 6.5 per cent remaining unbanked according to the Federal Deposit Insurance Corporation (FDIC). The number of underbanked households also dropped to 18.7 per cent in 2017 – representing approximately 48.9 million adults[9] in 24.2 million households. However, these figures only tell part of the US story. According to the Financial Health Network,[10] only 33 per cent of Americans are financially healthy, despite a decade-long economic boom. Moreover, financial health gaps persist across race and ethnicity. Women overwhelmingly bear the increase in this financial vulnerability, with 28 per cent of women[11] being financially healthy, compared to 40 per cent of men. This is a gap that has widened since 2018.

- Other developed economies have also experienced a lower number of unbanked populations. For example, the number of people without a current or basic transactional bank account in the **United Kingdom** reached an all-time low in 2017 at 1.23 million, according to the 2018–19 Financial Inclusion Report[12] by the UK Government. While the growing number of non-bank financial technology (FinTech) solutions play a critical role in improving financial access, the growing popularity of digital payments might inadvertently exclude those consumers who use cash only and have no access to digital payment services. An increasingly cashless society, combined with closing bank branches, will impact the more vulnerable segments of society – and those who live in rural areas. This movement may even be accelerated by the pandemic, which has prompted financial institutions to increasingly rethink their long-term branch strategy.

The economic issues associated with the global unbanked and the underbanked populations are multifaceted. Simply providing access will not automatically solve inequality and associated societal ills. We need greater efforts to provide financial education, more ways to bank remotely, and a renewed focus on the basic needs of those who are not served by our current system. There is an opportunity here not just for banking the unbanked, but also for the financial services ecosystem to truly serve the diverse needs of our global population – to make an impact on each individual, each family and each business.

Against this backdrop of unbanked individuals, there are also more than 200 million[13] micro, small and medium-sized enterprises that lack adequate financing, which has a ripple effect on their ability to contribute to local economies and local employment. The financial services industry – and the growing FinTech sector – have an opportunity to become more socially responsible, more connected to their customers and more focused on the common good. Financial inclusion should not be the end goal – it is a means to an end.

Establishing meaningful goals

The World Bank Group, together with private and public sector partners, set a target of attaining Universal Financial Access (UFA) by 2020, whereby 'adults globally will be able to have access to a transaction account or electronic instrument to store money, send and receive payments.'[14] With two-thirds of the world's unbanked adults having access to a mobile phone capable of money storage and money movement, increased digital adoption can make reaching global financial inclusion more likely. But achieving universal financial access won't be easy and is just the start of efforts to truly optimize.

The World Bank also established the broader goal of further reducing extreme poverty and balancing economic prosperity. With recent improvements in digital technology reducing the number of unbanked, moving beyond access involves acknowledging the importance and impact of FinTech solutions reaching further into populations that often rely solely on mobile phones for banking services. It underlines the importance of digitizing identity to make it easier to open accounts and allow for easier transfers of customer data, financial accounts and credit histories between geographies. This is critical to meet the needs of the unbanked – especially for temporarily or more permanently displaced populations.

The World Bank study states that 'since 2010, more than 55 countries have made commitments to financial inclusion, and more than 30 have either launched or are developing a national strategy.'[15] As these countries accelerate their efforts, governments need additional public/private coordination of their efforts to ensure financial access for the rural poor and women (the gender gap is present in poverty as well, as women are more impacted than men by more than 9 per cent) – both groups that make up large portions of those affected by global extreme poverty. These efforts must also include a focus on increasing financial literacy and consumer financial protection.

Financial institutions must be active partners in these efforts, working with the entities across the financial spectrum, regulators and non-governmental organizations (NGOs) that are focused on expanding financial inclusion in the markets they serve. As financial inclusion expands, financial health can then become a feature in more types of businesses. Working with banks and financial technology firms, businesses can focus their efforts on further modernizing their retail, credit and fraud platforms. This helps shift cash and paper-based financial instruments to digital, enabling the creation of financial histories that expands the use of transactional accounts and access to credit. This intention could result in every financial transaction from any business working to both improve financial health and act as a lever for broader inclusion.

In partnership, banks (and other businesses) must also 'support legal, regulatory and policy reforms, the design of government programmes to open up access to a range of financial services, including savings, insurance and credit, so that transaction accounts provide a pathway to full financial inclusion.' The World Bank study also concludes that banks must continue their efforts to leverage new technologies found through collaboration with FinTech firms, work to strengthen competition (both internal and external to the industry) and ensure a 'level playing field for banks, non-bank or non-traditional service providers, such as telecoms companies, FinTech firms, post offices, cooperatives and agent networks.'[16]

The question comes down to whether banks will focus on these opportunities, and what roles other types of business see themselves playing. With changes designed to open up the utility of banking, nearly every type of business can expand access to financial services, as well as help build the financial wellbeing of their customers with new value propositions.

Pushing a rock up a hill

US economist Milton Friedman made a strong argument for businesses' profitability in his *New York Times* article, 'The Social Responsibility of Business Is to Increase Its Profits'.[17] To this end, the banking business model has been incredibly successful – having historically more consistent profitability than nearly every industry. Compared to most businesses, banking's products and services revolve around something that is always in demand – the flow of money, the lifeblood of our global capitalist system. Global banks remain well capitalized and have posted record profits since the Great Recession ended a decade ago (and were better prepared for the economic black swan of the Covid-19 global pandemic because of new regulations). Why, then, should banking services providers look for ways to change their business model in order to better serve the underserved or the unbanked? Wouldn't that go against the Friedman doctrine of focusing on profit and maximizing returns to shareholders?

The simple answer is that you can do well by doing good. The industry should do more to drive towards full financial inclusion and more forms of financially focused optimization for all customers, as the opportunity is fairly significant (more on this later) and quite critical to its ability to retain future customer relationships. Achieving global financial inclusion combines the right thing to do – improving the lives of people in global society – with doing well – by maximizing long-term economic vitality. But changing an industry like financial services remains difficult, as banks are focused on metrics and the short-term profitability of their services – rather than the value and utility of them to more people in the communities they serve.

Large publicly traded financial-services firms are driven by fiscal quarters and financial results. This has created a generation of global executives focused on the short term, and financial incentives that have, frankly, made them very wealthy. Collective industry decisions dominated purely by profit are also rarely in their customer's interest, let alone the common good. Banking products and services, once relatively easy for consumers to digest, have evolved into a tangled nest of fees and complicated disclosures controlled by layers of siloed management. Somewhere in the transition of the last 25 years, customer value seems to have wandered into the wilderness at many of the largest global financial institutions. After centuries of the self-preservation of the banking business model, some form of correction was inevitable.

By the start of 2007, banking customers had become exotic segments, not centralized assets. With the advent of online and mobile technology further distancing the customer (generally under the guise of creating efficiencies), banking's business model continued to stack up increased profits created with increasingly complex financial services that had little to do with building customer value. Some of these, such as collateralized debt obligations (CDOs), enabled systematic risk that helped cause the Great Recession and permanently eroded trust in the industry. It's no wonder that serving the underserved became an afterthought, that regular customers' needs became secondary. The banking industry was fighting for its very survival. Post-recession, new challenges have emerged each year, especially in regard to technology and external private investment into the industry.

SPOTLIGHT ON A PIVOTAL YEAR

The financial services business model had remained relatively static over the past several centuries. It was primarily a personal-relationship-driven function of society that technology and circumstance slowly shifted towards more impersonal models . over time. The year 2007 was significant for the banking industry (and a number of others) for a lot of reasons. It saw the launch of M-Pesa in Kenya, the mobile-phone-based money-transfer and microfinancing platform from Safaricom; the initial Payment Services Directive (PSD) by the European Commission designed to regulate payment services and payment service providers; the launch of the iPhone from Apple, which ushered in the smartphone era; as well as the start of a very significant global recession.

All of these events have a great deal to do with the changes we've seen in financial services today and the move beyond just access towards optimization. The launch of M-Pesa (*Pesa* means money in Swahili) ushered in low-cost money movement to millions across East Africa and proved that other industries such as telecommunications could be instrumental in delivering banking services to the masses. The iPhone and smartphone-driven applications have fundamentally transformed our customer relationships, adding greater transparency to the role money plays in our lives, as well as adding a level of democratization by both demystifying and optimizing personal financial conditions.

The advent of the smartphone also started the concept that a mobile phone app could drive a business model as seemingly complex as a banking relationship. The Payment Services Directive was one of the first regulatory actions to initiate competition, innovation and open data across the European Union, and is seen by many as the precursor to what we call open banking today (more on this in the next chapter). The Great Recession made us question the value of the banking system while simultaneously creating a low-rate environment that acted as an incubator to an explosion of many of these global FinTech startups. The past decade has simply ushered in the greatest amount of innovation the financial services industry has ever seen. Why is this important to what we are seeing today? What does it mean for other industries, and what does it mean for financial inclusion and the common good?

It seems that putting a small but powerful mobile computer, connected to the rest of the world, into the hands of billions of people can create a great deal of change. Consider the banking business model that we have been discussing. Since the advent of the iPhone and the tangential rise of app stores, technology has started to pull the utility of banking towards its inevitable future as a feature. Compared to 2007, there are now tens of thousands of non-bank startups and corporations that offer banking services of different types through applications that people download on their smartphones. Banks no longer control the narrative at the heart of their business model.

Business-model evolution has occurred in many other industries as well: personal computing, telecom providers and mobile-phone manufacturers (look at how drastically companies such as phone-handset manufacturers Nokia and BlackBerry were impacted), movie and music production, the gaming industry, and many more. Why was the iPhone (and later, Android devices) so disruptive? Much of this has to do with the changes in the way consumers behave – how we bank, how we interact with brands and buy things, and how we consume information and go about our day. These changes have helped create billion-dollar companies (from ride-sharing companies such as Uber to service providers such as Ant Group and Tencent that have turned into superapps of consumption) and a new intimacy between business and customer.

Other industries have been impacted through this deeper connectivity between consumer and more personalized data-driven experiences: healthcare, transport and travel (hotels, airlines, train systems, mass transit, vacation rentals), photography, providers of business applications and directories (to connect both consumer to business and business to business) and commerce marketplaces (the physical superstore is now a mobile cornucopia of consumption). Technology has been the common disruptor; long-term market dynamics have been upended by more direct customer acquisition, broader transparency of price and value, and that ever-present 'buy now' button. The year 2007 (even more than the start of the internet and the world wide web earlier) started us down the path of more choice for nearly every conceivable good and service available on the planet.

While money remains a connection point for the utility of banking that enables these broader choices, it isn't necessarily the focal point of these more personal relationships. And this could become more problematic as our mobile march of global commerce continues. In the years since 2007, this increased connectivity has created opportunities for both new business creation and a host of financial challenges associated with overconsumption and wider use of credit for purchases.

This is why it is in the best interest of every industry to become more aware – and more involved – in the financial health of their customers. The more financially inclusive society is, the more financially healthier your community will be and the healthier your business environment will be.

That is why the Friedman doctrine calling for profitability at all costs – to maximize shareholder return – fails any test of common sense as it relates to the common good. The long-term viability of any business model is tied to the long-term physical and financial health of those individuals and businesses that make up the customers of any business, any industry.

The year 2007 initiated significant changes to the global economic dynamic, the system of supply and demand, and nearly every industry's business model. How have these changes impacted your business and your work, and how have they made you think differently about your responsibility to the broader community you serve? The more non-financial businesses understand how much the banking industry has changed, the more they can absorb the utility of banking (eg the facilitation of banking services such as payments, long-term savings and investments, access to credit) at a lower cost to the consumer and add it to the value of the products and services of their own endeavours. While banks themselves may eventually be replaced by technology and snippets of code, the need to facilitate banking endures.

Transparency is the core governance principle to make platforms more balanced and inclusive. By infusing transparency principles in our usage of digital technology, in progressive regulation and promoting novel bank business models, we can make the invisible hand visible again. PAOLO SIRONI, AUTHOR ON QUANTITATIVE FINANCE, DIGITAL TRANSFORMATION AND ECONOMICS THEORY.

How financial technology has changed

Technology has always played an important part in the financial services industry, dating back to the early 1900s with Fedwire – the electronic fund transfer system. Bank-issued charge cards came about in the 1940s, followed by the first credit card for widespread use: the Diners Club Card in 1950, and the American

Express in 1959. A magnetic stripe was added to the cards as a form of verification in 1960 – and credit cards, as we know them, more or less stayed the same until the arrival of RFID (radio frequency identification), which fuels the growth of touchless payments; and the EMV chip technology enables more secure transactions.

A great deal of innovation has taken place since then to enable payments beyond a physical card: from payment apps on smartphones or wearables to paying through facial recognition or your fingerprint. Along with credit cards, the introduction of an ATM (automated teller machine) at a branch of Barclays bank in London in 1967 marked the beginning of the brave new world of 'self-service' and 'automation'. Besides being able to automate the bank clerk's functions while not having to extend business hours, these machines allow banks to maintain or expand physical presence – without new branches – and without additional labour costs.

It would take several decades more before we hit the next evolution – one that provided consumers with further flexibility to conduct banking around the clock, anywhere they wanted. And that movement, along with growth of mobile payments, was fuelled by the proliferation of smartphones – especially the introduction of the iPhone in 2007, as previously discussed – which delivered a game-changing mobile experience that has altered our behavioural DNA, and banking's business model itself. In addition to new technologies, more changes for the banking industry were on their way.

The impact of FinTech

The past decade's recovery and low interest-rate environment have served as the perfect incubator for the rise of external financial technology investment and disruption. Banking's once formidable relationship with its customers is beginning to shift as the industry experiences the first waves of external innovation.

Thousands of startups, focused on areas from payments to credit to wealth creation and advice, have created a new dynamic. Both large technology platforms and small nimble startups deliver better value – or at least, more differentiated value – than most financial brands can deliver.

New global FinTech business models have emerged over the past two decades – from the US, UK, Africa, China, India, Southeast Asia and beyond. From personal finance to payment, from banking infrastructure to fraud, these FinTech startups have upended the world of financial services, changed consumer expectations of what can be done, and challenged incumbents to move beyond the status quo. Here are some notable examples of these pioneering startups:

- **Ant Group and Tencent**
  These two Chinese tech giants have not only upended how we think about financial services, but have also promoted financial inclusion in China to dramatically reduce the number of people that remain unbanked. They have done this through the use of digital applications on smartphones and transformed the country of 1.3 billion people into a near cashless society. They have each created a superapp ecosystem, enabling millions of users to conduct their lives via one app, from social media, ride hailing, e-commerce and delivery to payment, wealth management, insurance and much more.

- **M-Pesa, Transferwise, PayPal, Remitly and Venmo**
  Broadly speaking, these apps have changed how we move money between consumers and merchants, within and across borders. M-Pesa is a mobile-phone-based money-transfer service launched in 2007 by Vodafone for Safaricom and Vodacom, and has been credited for lifting 2 per cent of Kenyan households out of poverty. Meanwhile, PayPal is one of the earliest FinTech startups in the West and one of the best-known digital wallets; and Venmo (launched in 2009 and subsequently acquired by PayPal) is one of the most popular social-payment platforms. Transferwise and

Remitly have significantly reduced consumer costs associated with moving money cross-border and cross-currency. This has had a positive net impact on the global community.

- **Acorns, Betterment and Wealthfront**
  Robo-advisers such as Betterment and Wealthfront have driven down the cost for investment through automation, providing opportunities for new customer segments that were underserved by traditional investment firms owing to lack of assets. Separately, although the concept of 'rounding up a purchase' was pioneered by Bank of America, Acorns has popularized the concept of investing the spare change automatically with its 'Found Money' programme.

- **Lending Club, Kabbage, Prosper, Affirm and SoFi**
  Although the peer-to-peer lending model has transformed quite drastically since its inception, it has nevertheless changed the way we look at credit for a variety of needs. From personal loans to small business loans, from debt consolidation to student financing and mortgages, consumers and businesses no longer have to go to the bank to apply for a loan.

- **Square, Stripe and Klarna**
  It's profitable to be the *plumbing* in financial services (the systems and technology that enable transactions to flow more efficiently), especially in payments and data. Whether in physical stores, e-commerce or mobile apps, enabling easier payments and adding value around transaction data for both merchants and consumers has enabled new forms of value beyond banking.

- **Marqeta, MX, Yodlee and Plaid**
  A variety of FinTechs, including Plaid, Marqeta and MX, which are leveraging transaction data and new capabilities such as issuing cards and savings accounts, have helped other FinTech startups (and banking partners) develop new ways to onboard, assess and help customers with new services based on aggregated data and banking relationships.

SPOTLIGHT ON PAYPAL

No FinTech story is complete without mentioning PayPal, one of the earliest FinTech 'startups' and one of the best-known digital wallets. PayPal was established in December 1998 as Confinity, a company that developed security software for handheld devices. After a series of business and management changes, PayPal went Public IPO in 2002, and was acquired by eBay shortly after. It was eventually spun off from eBay in 2015.

According to PayPal's corporate website, the PayPal platform is 'available in more than 200 markets around the world, enabling consumers and merchants to receive money in more than 100 currencies, withdraw funds in 56 currencies and hold balances in their PayPal accounts in 25 currencies.'[18] In its Q4 2019 investor update, it reported 305 million active account holders, with 48 per cent being outside the US. The company has also taken an active interest in social innovations, and has introduced new solutions for the financially underserved. In keeping with its purpose-driven culture, PayPal reported that 50 per cent of its board are women or from under-represented ethnic groups – which is not a small achievement given the fact that most boards are dominated by white males.

Some of the company's more notable acquisitions include Braintree (and along with it Venmo, a popular social-mobile-payment platform), iZettle (also known as the Square of Europe), Zoom and Hyperwallet. Under the leadership of Dan Schulman, President and CEO of PayPal Holdings, PayPal has grown beyond being a payments platform. With its acquisition of Honey, a startup that helps consumers discover rewards and deals while shopping, PayPal has extended its footprint to include the purchase journey.

Dan Schulman once said that 'it is expensive to be poor.'[19] Managing and moving money shouldn't be a privilege of those who can afford it. Having a purpose as a company and being able to make a profit are not mutually exclusive. 'If you don't have a purpose as a company, you don't see your workers as your most valuable asset and you minimize your profitability.'[20] We are anxious to see how PayPal will continue to transform itself, as well as the industry.

Finding the soul of an industry

How can you define a shared sense of purpose – a unified mission – for an entire industry? Especially one like financial services, which is viewed with a high level of scepticism. In a poll on trust across 23 countries by Ipsos Global,[21] bankers ranked as the fourth least-trusted profession (41 per cent of respondents deeming them untrustworthy), faring better than only politicians (67 per cent), government ministers (57 per cent) and advertising executives (46 per cent). The most trustworthy profession? Scientists (11 per cent). How can an industry so critical to society be among its least trusted?

With the proper stakeholders from both private and public sectors, and with the right policy, this narrative around trust can change. Banking needs to find its soul once again, and through that process create a more inclusive financial-services system despite the challenges they face today. In Chapter Five we will take a deeper look at one such example.

Accenture estimates that banks could generate up to $380 billion in annual revenues by closing the small-business credit gap and bringing the unbanked and underbanked adults into the formal financial system.[22] It is also more than doing well by doing good.

Systemic financial exclusion results in greater poverty, shorter lifespans and an erosion of social equality. Closing the gap and moving towards full global financial inclusion will, quite frankly, elevate the human experience for our global population. At the very least, it will put us on the path towards more financial equality.

Purpose-driven business can sustainably co-exist with commercial success when profit becomes a means to an outcome that adheres to a set of morals, ethics and values. MANOJ GOVINDAN, VENTURE BUILDER

Hearts and mindsets

To embrace the principles of *Beyond Good*, business leaders must work together to turn hearts and mindsets towards action. Collectively, the financial-services industry can fundamentally make the utility of banking better, more inclusive and fairer to everyone – because it impacts every sector and every business. The more we think about how banking affects us, the more we can improve it.

While the influx of FinTech startups was seen by many as a way to democratize the economic power held by the banking industry, unconscious biases have largely driven innovation and solutions that remain designed to generate revenue rather than improve financial wellbeing and financial lives. Banking practitioners must aim to improve our communities by getting their financial institutions to be actively involved in in-person financial-education efforts designed to improve financial health. Banking and FinTech technologists should not accept restrictions from legacy solutions; rather they should build new ones that move beyond access towards true optimization. Agents of change must work with all the stakeholders, including banks, startups, corporate partners, regulators and policymakers to make this happen.

Working as one, financial services will absolutely achieve global financial inclusion and start to eradicate larger issues such as extreme poverty, and help those most impacted by the unequal access to money and long-term wealth creation within society. Not only is it necessary, but it is also achievable. And it will happen within our lifetimes.

CHAPTER FOUR

A renewed business model

Every Company Will Be a FinTech Company.[1] ANGELA
STRANGE, ANDREESSEN HOROWITZ

The tail wagging the dog

As we discussed in the last chapter, the financial services industry is changing rather dramatically. This has implications for nearly every industry, as the utility of banking is separated from the value it provides. The financial services industry is being systematically unbundled, with individual pieces of the customer relationship being served by very specialized startups offering simpler-to-understand and easier-to-use products and services. Bankers fret about these startups nibbling away at their most profitable customers. Revised business models and technologies have the potential to dismantle core areas of the industry's traditional business model and more critically, connectivity to the underlying customer value proposition. For many working within banking, the pace of FinTech innovation is unsettling, perhaps even terrifying. Will innovation drive more inclusive practices, moving towards a model that goes *Beyond Good*?

Very few areas of banking have been untouched by the sheer amount of technology innovation. Along with mobile technologies, emerging technologies from cloud computing to blockchain, from artificial intelligence to machine learning, from the rise of digital delivery to automated services, have simply transformed the financial services industry. These are all fuelled by venture-capital investment into FinTech startups, which have been a significant part of these changes to our business model. Banks have learned from these investments too – a third of FinTech investments involve a corporate venture team, many from banks themselves. This has significantly impacted the way in which banks have looked at integrating technology into their brands, and has paved the way for many FinTech mergers and acquisitions in recent years.

Payment players are changing global access to how people send and store money. These include, for example, M-Pesa in Kenya, which, as mentioned earlier, provides access to payments and microcredits; WeChat and Alipay, which leverage QR codes to enable consumers to buy goods; and bKash in Indonesia, Transferwise in the UK and Remitly in Mexico and the Philippines, which make it possible for immigrants and expatriates to move money across borders at lower costs. According to the latest McKinsey report on global payments, in 2019, 'Cross-border payments totalled $130 trillion, generating payments revenues of $224 billion (up 4 per cent from the previous year).'[2] Tackling this opportunity is incredibly important to broadening inclusion and reducing the costs of moving money for all users of these services.

Large technology platforms are also getting much more involved in expanding access to financial services, from Google,

Apple, Facebook and Amazon to Ant Group, Baidu, Grab, Line and others. Money is an essential part of our daily life and activities and these platforms are embedding it further into the background through digital payments and money movement.

Globally minded challenger banks – sometimes called neobanks, and defined as new digital direct banks that aren't always banks but sometimes rely on bank partners – are sprouting up in a dozen geographies and are challenging traditional banks for market share. They offer simplified banking experiences – spending and savings accounts, along with optimization to help people improve their personal financial wellbeing. All of these efforts impact how we look at the banking model itself. What is a bank now, if not a simple app? What is a banking relationship, if not a relationship with a technology provider?

Banks are being unbundled by startups that are singularly focused and driving efficiencies in new ways for each part of banking's traditional business. After a decade of unbundling, banks are now attempting to re-establish customer relationships through new services or partnering with startups to add customer value – in essence, rebundling banking in new ways. In the long run, is this a good thing or a bad thing for society? Is it a good thing for the underserved? The results have been promising, but it will depend on how well the system is regulated and allowed to safely innovate. Either way, technology is driving the biggest change to the financial services model in its history, and it is a genie that you cannot put back in the bottle.

What's the lesson for other industries? Are they being unbundled in similar fashion? From Boeing to GE, Honda to Porsche, Adidas to Zara, and Chanel to L'Oréal – you cannot name a brand or industry that isn't being impacted by the change in consumer habits, the shift in purchase behaviours or the change in customer relationships. Massive marketplaces are challenging the once direct relationship between producer and consumer in a way that is similar to what is happening to banking. These marketplaces include Amazon, PayPal, eBay, Mercado Libre, AliExpress, Rakuten, Taobao, Walmart and JD.com. No geography is excluded, no business model immune. The way we consume just about everything is impacted by technology, even how goods get to our doorsteps.

The unbundling of traditional financial services has crept deeper into our global supply chains. Shipping companies, such as APM-Maersk, MSC-Mediterranean and Cosco, are being impacted by demands for new forms of payment. These are replacing centuries-old processes involving letters of credit to validate exchange of goods. Payments are potentially being replaced by blockchain-fuelled technology and smart contracts to verify the condition of shipments, including verifying the source and authenticity of goods shipped in order to reduce counterfeiting and impacts on human health (with regard to the legitimate sources of foods and medicines); tracking the condition of goods during shipment (continual monitoring of temperature, humidity, movement and other factors); and the release of payments between producer, seller and shipper in a more expedient manner. Companies innovating in this space include Voltron, Skuchain, Marco Polo and we.trade. Banking is far from alone in experiencing these forces of change.

The next step of the journey

The journey from unbundling to rebundling and back has been a formidable one. In the past decade, emerging technologies and the pace of innovation have driven changes throughout the banking industry at an unprecedented rate. FinTech startups have matured from novelty to niche and moved towards becoming considerable contenders by entering the mainstream in major markets around the world. It is not surprising, then, that while Covid-19 has brought venture capital deal activity to recent lows around the world, later-stage megadeals have continued to gain share as the ecosystem matures (according to the CB Insights 'State of FinTech Q2 '20 Report').[3]

Emerging markets, notably China and India, have led the way with companies such as Alibaba, Tencent and Paytm. The FinTech consumer-adoption rate stands high at 87 per cent for both India and China, according to the EY Global FinTech Adoption Index,[4] compared to 71 per cent in the UK and 46 per cent in the US. Money-transfer and payment FinTechs consistently top the list when it comes to consumer awareness, from peer-to-peer payments to mobile payments and money transfer.

Although the movement towards the ability to bank anywhere is inevitable, the path to transformation varies from one region to the next – and very different models have evolved within each region. While challenger banks have flourished especially in Europe, thanks to an open banking framework, outside of the incumbent banks and FinTech startups, a new force of disruption has emerged. From Alipay and WeChat Pay in China, to Grab and Gojek in Southeast Asia, banking services are increasingly being provided by big technology companies via smartphones and without human bankers – and consumers are adopting them en masse.

Banks of the future will increasingly be run by technology, driven by consumers who are spending more time than ever on their mobile devices and have grown accustomed to the seamless experience with technology companies. We are living in a digital era where customers rarely visit bank branches and mostly prefer to bank and shop from the comfort of their home or as they go about their day, when they want it and how they want it. Mobile banking has moved from reporting the past towards focusing on predicting the future.

To build new value, financial institutions must reimagine banking itself within the context of our daily lives, our routines, our needs, our desires and their impact on our future. They need to create an ecosystem of partnerships to improve their core offerings – as no one can do everything well on their own. They must modernize the infrastructure and adopt changes in architecture in order to speed up the product delivery cycle. Knowing who your customers are and generating insights based on past behaviour will no longer be sufficient. Being customer-centric is about leveraging the power of advanced data analytics to predict what the customer needs and when they need it; and it must be about developing positive financial actions to improve their outcome, rather than just profiting from it. Just as modern technology companies have made it frictionless to spend money, so must we innovate and leverage technology to reshape the future – a future where people can have the opportunity to build wealth and attain long-term financial security, regardless of where they come from, and regardless of their demographics and social circles.

This movement from traditional providers to new challengers, and from slower, more lumbering incumbents towards technology-driven upstarts isn't only being seen in financial services, of course. Tangentially to banking, the protections provided by traditional service providers in areas such as insurance (companies such as Berkshire Hathaway, AXA and China Life Insurance) are being challenged by a slew of startups, including Lemonade, Roost, Slice, Clover, Oscar, CoverWallet, TrueAccord, Trov and many more. These smaller, nimbler companies are offering quick onboarding and comparatives to existing customers of other providers, and in many cases, offer better price points for the same services. Their efficiencies are driven by technology, smaller teams and near-zero customer-facing physical footprint.

Perhaps sensing the potential threat of a tech platform replicating the superapp model from the East and bypassing the banks, JPMorgan Chase has indicated that they would provide e-wallet capabilities to e-commerce and gig economy companies such as Lyft and Amazon, to enable them to offer virtual bank accounts and financial services such as car loans to their drivers. This model would resemble that of Gojek, based in Indonesia, which started as a technology company providing ride-hailing services, before being transformed into one of the largest super-apps in the region, giving entrepreneurs and small businesses access to banking services, from payments to loans. Such an arrangement would have been worth JPMorgan Chase exploring – to address the potential threat of disintermediation by conceding some control in the payments process.

There truly isn't any industry where startups and technology advances aren't impacting incumbents. The real question is, is the value that these companies deliver that much better? Are their business models that much more transparent? Are the price points and associated costs of shifting providers better for communities? Does the introduction of alternatives in any given industry improve the common good?

SPOTLIGHT ON PROPEL VENTURE PARTNERS

Propel Venture Partners, previously an in-house venture arm known as BBVA Ventures, is an independent venture firm backed by BBVA. Set up as a Small Business Investment Company (SBIC) and licensed by the Small Business Administration, the US fund is limited to investment in US corporations only. In parallel, the firm has also set up a European fund to invest internationally.

The firm invests in companies that are focused on the technology as opposed to the 'fin' in FinTech, according to Ryan Gilbert, General Partner of Propel Venture Partners and FinTech veteran. Some of its portfolio companies include Hippo (home insurance), Guideline (401k for small business), Steady (platform for gig economy workers) and Charlie (advisory chatbot for consumers).

The investment in Steady is particularly interesting and timely, reflecting a changing trend in the nature of employment. And as we have witnessed especially in the West, the gig economy sector is severely underserved by incumbent financial institutions. With a mission to build a better financial future for the growing gig workforce, Steady is an online community for gig workers where

---

they can find jobs, seek financial advice and save money with deals. According to the company's own data, over 78 per cent of its 2 million members do not have an easy way to earn $500 to cover an emergency prior to joining the platform, a common challenge among independent workers. Early results seem promising: Steady reported that its members earn approximately $4,000 more per year with the platform.

With more workers than ever relying on gig work as their primary income, solutions such as Steady that can help contingent workers plan and manage their finances better will likely gain prominence. We will go into more details in the next chapter.

The work you do needs to allow you to look yourself in the mirror, and say, I have done something good and meaningful. RYAN GILBERT, PROPEL VENTURE PARTNERS

According to the 2020 State of FinTech Report by CB Insights, global FinTech funding reached $3.4 billion across 141 deals in June 2020, with the sector overseeing a flurry of IPO filings.[5] While wealthtech and banking infrastructure companies have been particularly active, embedded finance has been gaining traction around the world as financial technology is increasingly being integrated across non-banking sectors. Big tech companies in particular are focusing on payment products as a way to evolve new models of financial services. A look at two banks offers a glimpse of what the future might hold.

SPOTLIGHT ON GOLDMAN SACHS

An example of the old guard learning new tricks is Goldman Sachs, an institution with over 150 years of history, which has been on its own digital transformation journey in recent years. Goldman made a push into savings accounts and credit cards via the launch of Marcus, Goldman's consumer bank, in 2016. Its vision is to be the leading consumer bank of the future, addressing the spending, borrowing and saving needs of millions of customers and helping them take control of their financial lives. It entered the credit-card business with the Apple Card launch in August 2019, and has since rolled out a mobile app for Marcus, leveraging the technology behind Clarity Money, a personal finance FinTech startup purchased by Goldman in 2018. According to the presentations from Goldman Sachs' 2020 Investor Day, the Marcus platform has gained about 5 million customers, garnered $60 billion in deposits and $7 billion in loan/card balances to date.[6] As part of its digital finance strategy, Goldman has indicated that it intends to leverage what has been built for Marcus and create an external cloud platform for other digital banks and FinTech companies, externalizing its core technology platform – a model similar to that used by Amazon and its Amazon Web Services (AWS).

Another interesting pillar to note at the backdrop of its digital transition is the acquisition of United Capital, a wealth management FinTech startup now rebranded as Goldman Sachs Personal Financial Management. A combined wealth-management solution leveraging synergy between Ayco, a financial counselling company acquired in 2003, and United Capital, is expected to grow Goldman's high-net-worth and mass-affluent client base. The firm has also indicated that wealth-management capability and checking accounts will be added to the Marcus platform.

The Apple Card rollout is notable for its marketing campaign that reads: 'Created by Apple – not a bank.' Will this be the future model for others to follow? Will that future involve a bank?

On a different continent, another renowned financial institution with over 160 years of history is also betting its future on digital transformation and the FinTech ecosystem.

SPOTLIGHT ON BBVA

With more than 160 years of history, BBVA (based in Spain) is the largest financial institution in Mexico, with a strong leadership position in the Spanish market along with presence in 30 countries. Understanding the need to drive mobile solutions, the bank has invested heavily in digital transformation, with 60 per cent digital-customer penetration, according to the BBVA 2Q20 corporate presentation.[7] The bank has also earned the top spot in Forrester's Global Mobile Banking App Reviews,[8] and continues to experience growth in customer satisfaction, as indicated by its top Net Promoter Score.[9]

BBVA is among the few banks that has actively sought partnerships in the FinTech ecosystem early on to create a diverse digital business portfolio, as follows:

- Through its Venture Creation Partnership with Anthemis, the venture-building studio, it provides startups with access to mentoring and support services alongside working capital. One of the first companies created through this partnership was UK-based income-smoothing FinTech startup Wollit, which aims to provide a subscription-based cash-flow product for gig workers living without the financial security of a stable income.

- As discussed earlier, BBVA launched Propel Ventures as an independent venture arm after shutting off its in-house venture arm, to scout for opportunities at the intersection of technology and finance.

- In addition to investing in Propel, BBVA has also acquired or made direct investments in various FinTech startups, including Atom, the UK's first mobile-only bank; Hippo, an online home-insurance provider; Prosper, a digital lender; Personal Capital, a wealth-management adviser; Simple, a US neobank; and Taulia, a supply-chain finance company.

- Through its Open Platform, BBVA offers banking-as-a-service for incumbents and FinTechs, such as Digit and Wise, with a suite of APIs that includes identity verification (KYC), payments, account origination, card issuance and notifications.

As consumers are becoming more accustomed to conducting transactions online, providing digital-banking capabilities is no longer a nice-to-have, but a must-have. To stay competitive, financial institutions must find ways to add value to consumers' lives. One way that banks can do this is by building an ecosystem of partners and leveraging their respective offerings. The road to digital is not easy, but BBVA's success provides a blueprint for others to follow.

Digging new moats, taming new hedgehogs

Incumbents have been reacting to these new models with renewed energy and focus, both deploying aggressive investment and acquisition strategies to remain competitive and creating new defensible moats of efficient and rapidly deployable ecosystems. As we discussed with the examples of BBVA and Goldman Sachs, the new way that older brands remain nimble is through investing in, digesting or copying the competition. Will this end up creating new hedgehogs in line with the *Good to Great* model, or will they produce more value for a greater number of constituents more in line with what we espouse in *Beyond Good*?

That existing firms want to remain relevant is not surprising, but what are the greater costs associated with these aggressions when it comes to overall innovation, consumer value or the opportunity for advancing the common good? Brands like Facebook are notorious for their aggressive behaviour; they gobbled up brands such as Instagram and WhatsApp, and attempted to destroy competition from Snapchat and TikTok through outright copying or political means. Are deeper moats the real answer? Are new hedgehogs that curl up into balls and show their defensive spikes the right direction?

Perhaps we need new forms of olive branches in business, where we find rising tides that lift up all boats. The more open, expanding ecosystem may be the best way to benefit more communities. This model is probably best explained by talking about it as a form of logistics first. Large global manufacturers of different goods and services – automakers such as BMW and Toyota, electronic manufacturers such as Hitachi and Samsung, large marketplaces such as Amazon, pharmaceutical companies such as Cardinal Health, and food, beverage and agricultural providers such as Cargill, Coca-Cola, ConAgra and Nestlé – all have vast supply-chain and logistic ecosystems that tie all of their raw goods together to their end production facilities, their shipment providers and their end retail partners. They are tied together through complicated networks of physical goods, partners and technology that ensure their ongoing ability to provide quality end products to their consumers.

When you look at the supply-chain models of individual businesses, you will see a complicated mix of interdependencies that technology holds together. You will also see a shared vision of values. Sometimes the most important lesson in business isn't trying to win, it's in ensuring everyone wins. The best, most sustainable ecosystems in the world have this shared set of values. They continually seek transparency, are adaptable to the needs of both the local markets of raw materials and conditions of labour and its reward, and are cognizant of and compliant to the changing expectations of end customers. These are the companies truly built to last – the companies focused on shared values present throughout its supply chain, the businesses that grow by expanding a shared reward over a collapsing defensible moat.

Apple is a great example of this. They lead through their complicated supply chain from their raw-materials contractors and suppliers to their chips, semiconductors and other components of their phones to the conditions on factory floors in Shenzhen. While no company gets everything right – just ask clothing manufacturers like Gap or auto manufacturers like

Volkswagen – the real winners of each industry see their business as an opportunity to improve each community it has a privilege to serve. Our global connected world is just that – an opportunity for businesses and business leaders to create ecosystems of value for more communities.

Large or small, we create our own ecosystem that drives the flywheel for all sustainable businesses, defining our value chain to our customers. From ConAgra to Coca-Cola, from Apple to Amazon, knowing what you do well and continually improving your logistics ensures relevancy. Going back to financial services, open banking should be viewed in this way as well.

Open banking and the battle for data

In the age of algorithms, how can we leverage data to truly engage with our customers and provide real value for them, be there at the right place, at the right time? How do financial institutions differentiate themselves beyond convenience? The key to unlocking this is data. Your personal data.

Until recently, a consumer's financial data was centrally held within their financial institution. But this has started to change with the implementation of various open banking initiatives that have evolved through the past decade and launched within recent years across the globe. Could this be the checkmate for the traditional banking industry? The ultimate trojan horse that will unbundle all of banking itself? Regulations aimed at facilitating sharing of consumer financial data with third-party technology companies and open APIs have helped challenger banks flourish in Europe. More have taken to applying for full banking licences, allowing them to take deposits or write loans. Open-banking-driven business models could fundamentally change the banking business model as we know it today. It means that any licensed provider can be a trusted part of the global financial system. That could change everything.

But will it in the end? Despite the growing popularity of these new FinTech entities, it is still too soon to tell if they are truly able to disrupt the high-street banks. Despite billions in venture capital funding, many lack a clear path to a profitable, self-sustaining business built to last as long as most banks. Time will tell.

Meanwhile, in the US, the incumbent banks have largely remained dominant, with even greater concentration among the largest institutions. Regulatory changes also appear to be far off, compared to its European counterparts. However, it is becoming apparent that the future of banking will be driven by open business models and APIs, as demonstrated by Mastercard's acquisition of Finicity, Visa's acquisition of Plaid, Lending Club's acquisition of Radius Bank, and Intuit's acquisition of Credit Karma. The common theme of all these recent land grabs is access to data, which is as important as oil was in the industrial revolution.

Future success will come to those companies that build the most trust with their customers, gain access to the most relevant data, and deliver the most value from it. And we are just at the beginning stages of this data-driven revolution. It is most apparent in the Far East with the rise of superapps, where many aspects of a consumer's life are increasingly being served by a single entity.

The rise of the superapps

According to CB Insights, as of June 2020, there are 66 VC-backed FinTech unicorns (companies valued at more than $1 billion) worth a combined $248 billion, including 37 in the US, 12 in Asia, 12 in Europe, 3 in South America and 2 in Australia.[10] In recent years, China has produced numerous fast-growing technology giants, including Alibaba, Baidu, JD, PingAn and Tencent. From how we communicate to how we pay, these companies have challenged the norms of how we live, work and play, as well as what we should expect in this new digital era. Tech giants such as Ant Group (an affiliate of Alibaba) and Tencent are years ahead of their rivals in the rest of the world, and handle more payments than all global credit-card transactions combined. They have become so ubiquitous in China that even homeless people on the streets use QR codes to ask for money from those that pass by. Citizens of cities like San Francisco and Berkeley should take note.

In parallel, digital payments have been growing in India – thanks in part to the demonetization policy of the government in late 2016 to remove most paper currency in circulation. As mentioned in earlier chapters, 69 per cent of the adult population now have bank accounts.[11] Great strides continue to be made, from alternative lending to formalization of digital ID and other ways to modernize banking. The Unified Payments Interface (UPI) has seen mass adoption by big tech players from Google to Paytm and WhatsApp. The Aadhaar identity platform is one of the key pillars of 'Digital India,' and the Aadhaar programme is now the largest biometrics-based identification system in the world. This series of efforts undertaken by the Indian government and regulators serve to create a favourable environment for FinTech innovation as the country continues to push for progress.

Elsewhere in Southeast Asia, Grab and Gojek have transformed themselves from ride-hailing companies into two large superapp ecosystems in the region, providing logistics, payments and entertainment services to millions of drivers, merchants and consumers. These two platforms provide microentrepreneurs, who are otherwise unbanked, with access to financial services, as well as new ways to grow and thrive.

With over 9 million microentrepreneurs on Grab's platform,[12] in a region where 'only 27 per cent of adults have formal bank accounts and only 33 per cent of businesses have access to proper financing',[13] there are ample opportunities to advance financial inclusion. While such platforms are fuelling the growth towards a cashless future, the rise of digital is not without its perils.

Are we becoming more exclusionary as we march down the path towards digital? Consider the following statistics from the UK, where 2 million people in Great Britain still don't have a bank account according to the Financial Inclusion Commission (FIC), and 8 million adults would struggle to cope in a cashless society largely owing to the country's poverty levels.

By eliminating cash as a payment option, are we inadvertently marginalizing consumers who are unbanked and do not have access to credit- or debit-driven accounts? Many of these consumers are low-income and immigrant households, the homeless and those who live in rural areas without access to the internet; they must be given the option to choose the payment options that they want – digital or otherwise.

SPOTLIGHT ON ZESTMONEY

ZestMoney is an Indian FinTech that extends consumer credit through merchants using a proprietary AI-based decision engine, leveraging data points from the consumers' digital footprint. The solution provides dynamic credit limits based on affordability, and it is tailored for households instead of individuals, taking into account the social dynamics and needs of the Indian market.

While the majority of financial products in India are still designed for prime customers with proof of salary and an established credit score, there is an untapped market for those consumers who don't have formal financing options. This includes the need for affordable solutions to help consumers 'buy now, pay later' and help them build long-term credit. ZestMoney also educates consumers about their credit score through its platform so that they can better maintain a long-term financial relationship rather than being penalized for being consistently transactional alone.

ZestMoney's innovative technology and efforts to make affordable digital finance accessible led to its selection as a 2020 Technology Pioneer by the World Economic Forum.[14] As Lizzie Chapman, CEO and co-founder of ZestMoney told us, its ultimate aim is to drive financial inclusion for the masses, especially for the ones who are not part of the formal credit system and have insufficient credit history. In a market like India, FinTechs can use technology to address barriers such as location, language and income by shaping consumer behaviour and improving financial outcomes.

There is a growing need to provide services to demographics previously left behind by the formal financial-services system. As our lives are becoming increasingly digital, companies can develop innovative and inclusive business models using new alternative data. The ability to create significant and unprecedented impact and help millions of people achieve their dreams through affordable, transparent EMI solutions is what drives the ZestMoney team forward.

The challenge is for all of us to act in a similarly ethical and responsible way, with the best interests of the consumer in mind. This is how we will improve conditions for more people in our communities.

With great power comes great responsibility; lending is easy, responsible lending is hard. LIZZIE CHAPMAN, CEO & CO-FOUNDER OF ZESTMONEY

Humans versus algorithms

How do we ensure greater inclusion and fairer outcomes when more decisions are increasingly being made by algorithms? How do we ensure that technology will help protect the rights of the people, especially those who are underprivileged?

When algorithms decide how we experience the news, suggest who we connect with on social networks and recommend what we should buy, how much of each decision is really our own? What is the future of humanity beyond algorithms, data and code?

We need answers to these questions more urgently than ever. To be fair, the question of ethics and bias existed before the dawn of artificial intelligence and algorithms. Ethics is both personal and contextual, and unconscious bias is deeply rooted in our upbringing. However, having algorithms mistake your choice of music or online purchase is one thing; having it turn down your loan or misjudge your investment preferences is another – with far more dire consequences.

Imagine when 'access to credit is gauged not just by our credit history, but by the friends in our social media circle; when our worthiness is determined through an algorithm with little to no transparency or human recourse; when our eligibility for insurance is determined by machine-learning systems based on our DNA and our perceived digital profiles.'[15] Whose values will the algorithm be based on then? Whose ethics will be embedded in these calculations? How do we preserve transparency and fairness and ensure that we are working with a glass box instead of a black box?

While the banking industry continues to transform itself and society, we must remember to safeguard the fundamental rights of all people. As we seek new ways to leverage technology to expand access and make the financial services system work better, we must also stay vigilant about the potential unintended consequences, and that we have the necessary guardrails in place to ensure the data is not biased and the outcomes are fair. Even though our past might be biased, we have a chance to create a more inclusive future – one that treats each one of us with greater dignity.

When we consider all currencies such as sustainability, responsibility, goodwill – profits cannot be achieved without true purpose. JOYEETA DAS, CEO AT GYANA

Embedded finance

As technology continues to reduce friction, banking will become more embedded in our day-to-day life. What a bank is and what a bank does will most likely continue to evolve in the years to come. It is estimated that at minimum, humans and machines will generate 175 zettabytes of data over the next five years alone.[16] How will our financial future be reimagined with such an abundance of data and unparallelled computational power? Will machines be able to predict what we need and when we need it, based on our behaviour and historical data? What insights will the virtual assistants be able to glean from our conversations? Will technology help us make better decisions and enable us to attain a more secure financial future? Will the bottom 10 per cent finally be able to access the same services as the top 1 per cent? What is more apparent than ever is that we are all intertwined in this global economy, and the banking business model is capable of much more.

Today, we see more and more examples of how banking as a function has started to disappear. Within the world of financial services, venture capital driven FinTech startups and large technology platforms we like to say that banking is becoming 'embedded'. Embedded simply means being surrounded by another function or feature. One can now imagine a world where nearly every aspect of traditional banking is an invisible feature of another industry's product or service experience. Welcome to the age of embedded finance. This is a truly fascinating development in an industry that has made tremendous profit out of being very present in both the tangible and intangible aspects of our financial lives. With the advent of and decade-long trend towards the unbundling of financial services, from payments through credit to wealth management, it is interesting to see both open and embedded banking further loosening banking's grip on its global customer base.

Will the rise of the superapp model and more deeply embedded banking usher in new levels of democratized access to financial services and further the quest for full financial inclusion? As financial services become increasingly fragmented, we must look back for clues about where we are headed next and where the biggest opportunities to serve the financial needs of more people might lie. Do you remember what banking used to be like? There was a time not too long ago when most primary functions we did with any financial-services brand was bundled together in a single relationship. This fusion of day-to-day banking, savings, credit, and often investments, was tied to a physical bank branch, and often a single person or small group, who acted as our personal banker. Banking was something we did at a particular place and at very distinct times. Its evolution towards the industry we know today really started with the introduction of consumer payments.

As the industry expanded its digital footprint into credit cards, ATM cards, instalment loans and more electronic options to store, move and access money, banking became much more mobile and less reliant on physical currency and paper cheques. Jumping forward several decades with the introduction of voice banking, online banking and mobile banking – accelerated by the introduction of the truly 'smart' phone in 2007 – the level of convenience and wider use of technologies such as APIs, AI/ML and cloud computing are among the many reasons banking is being widely upended. A model once full of friction has become truly frictionless.

The future of payments is here

As traditional banking services are becoming a utility, developers can now simply drop the code of any banking activity – whether onboarding, identity, payments, credit or investment – directly into their application workflow and make banking itself fade into the background. New business models have emerged, including the superapps of several large technology firms in China and Southeast Asia, which allow consumers and small businesses to combine day-to-day life needs and business functions into one single application. Will this be the new global model?

This change in dynamics allows businesses to move the focus from simply conducting transactions towards building more long-term relationships. Over the next decade consumers will continue to demand more convenient functionality and frictionless experiences. The ability to be in the right place at the right time – supporting consumers and retailers alike – to be where they want, how they want it and when they want it – cannot be understated.

Nor can the symbiotic relationship that develops between consumers and businesses that are focused on a similar goal – connectivity and alignment. Consumers and users of the superapps want to combine the convenience of having all their financial and non-financial needs met in one place, and businesses look to solidify more committed customers as part of their focus on growth. In the interim, people's financial wellbeing improves as their goals start to align with the companies they interact with. This flexibility and alignment, offered by the likes of superapps that are so prevalent in Asia, starts with transactional connectivity.

In the digital finance world of Alipay, for example, payments are merely the pipes – and a means to an end, empowering the digital lives of over 1 billion everyday consumers through everything from food delivery and transport to entertainment and digital finance, among other services. This is all fuelled by an ecosystem of data and connectivity designed to improve their customers' daily lives.

The role of the platform, with its abundance of data, is becoming increasingly crucial in a growing economy heavily reliant on small and micro businesses, long an underserved segment of the market. As demand for credit, investment and insurance grows, the platform can assess risks, streamline and deploy personalized experiences, and leverage insights facilitated by a hyper-connected ecosystem.

Imagine the platform as a physical machine, where every user behaviour, purchase and interaction feeds the algorithms, fine-tuning every decision made, and generating petabytes of data centred on real-time human connectivity. Through this data, there is now the capacity to offer personalization and optimization on a scale never seen before. But what does this look like in practice? How can the machine enhance financial wellbeing, starting with money movement?

When we think about how money moves today, the global machine of disjointed systems is far from optimized. Part of this is because the machine isn't truly connected in the way that we think. Sure, just like the way data flows through the interconnected system of the internet, the pipes that move money are certainly connected, but the value of the information running through it isn't optimized for our consumption. It seems logical then that a connected system of money movement mapped to the daily lives and activities of consumers and businesses would perform the more important task of truly meeting wants and needs. And what happens when that centralized engine learns to optimize our finances?

The dawn of ambient banking

The dawn of ambient banking is what we are seeing today with the superapp platforms in the East, each one creating a perpetual learning machine designed to meet the needs of multiple parties at once, all the while learning from itself how to perform that task better. We are only witnessing the very beginning of a long march towards the disappearance of financial services.

What happens when nearly every function that CB Insights identifies as the FinTech 250[17] is rolled into one application powered by a centralized engine? What happens when the goals of these companies are embedded in a single entity, their needs no longer dictated by a multitude of shareholders and venture-backed investors? What happens when the viewpoint and purview of all these companies are brought into one view? This makes the future much more compelling.

So where will we go from here? How will the model of embedded finance evolve? From the US (eg Amazon, Apple, Facebook) to India (eg WhatsApp, Paytm, PhonePe) and Latin America (eg Movile, Nubank, Rappi), where will we see the most promise? This is where embedded finance gets interesting. When you combine the functionality of the superapp – the ability to understand and learn from the daily experiences of more than a billion people using the app every day – you start to align more longer-term goals with daily activities.

By analysing daily spend, you have the ability to better facilitate savings and investments, to help build additional wealth over the long term. As you enable just-in-time infusions of credit, you create new opportunities for businesses to quickly meet the changing needs of their customers. As you connect real-time consumer behaviour to the small and medium-sized businesses that can fulfil them, you are creating a flywheel of impact on the financial lives of everyone.

When banking becomes more ambient, the pure profit motive of banks changes. While the superapp model connects buyer and seller, consumer and business, it connects the goals of each and creates a machine of perpetual motion towards more inclusive business practices that can improve the human condition. This is why removing the historical business model of financial services from the physical act of banking is an imperative. This is the path towards global financial inclusion that goes beyond access and the existing paradigm and moves the industry forward.

As the function and utility of the banking business model evolves, how can we ensure that new forms of data will drive us towards greater inclusion? While technology companies may look at banking as simply an extension of their existing business – to embed 'banking' services as part of existing strategies of monetization around data – banking is different. Banking still requires great trust. Through entrusting savings, investments, day-to-day bills and payments, what people use credit for, money means more to people because it represents their ability to cover their most basic needs.

The majority of people are likely to care less about personal data being used by technology companies as long as they gain some sort of service they desire, or convenience that wasn't there before. But money – and the data around money – is different. Money flows through people's lives enabling both their lifestyle and a physical embodiment of their values. Companies that look at the activities around money as a function of their source of profit and engagement must be cautious and thoughtful about the broader ramifications.

Embedding finance requires a holistic approach to tie the function of money into the value system of a person's life, which is more than a feature of someone's application workflow. So the difference between open banking and data sharing and a more holistic embedded finance is just that – a way to embed bank-like services to better enable the lives we want to lead; it carries our hopes and ambitions and transfers the bottom line from a banking provider to the longer-term goals of the individual.

The promise of embedded banking is in the shifting focus of the financial-services business model from the profitability of the banking provider to the long-term financial wellbeing of the consumer and business provider. The goals of any one company should not be more important than one that betters the community, that improves society as a whole and includes empathy for everyone it can serve.

FinTech is like any other technology; it amplifies our intentions. The purpose of FinTech is to amplify the very best of our intentions – to help everyone build financially healthier lives. ALEX JOHNSON, DIRECTOR OF PORTFOLIO MARKETING AT FICO

Empathy-driven business models

The evolution towards a more inclusive society will require new business models and new forms of empathy driven into existing business practices. It propels companies to use their resources and influence to tackle social issues and give back to the communities they serve. There are good reasons for businesses to consider alternatives to business as usual. It turns out you can do well while doing good.

Here are a few examples of business models that go *Beyond Good*. Starting outside of financial services, empathy-driven business models are leveraging technology to address various community needs and concerns about health and wellness. Companies such as Impossible and Beyond (meatless meats), Purple Carrot (vegetable-based food delivery) and Bulletproof (Rainforest Alliance certified coffee and wellness drinks) are addressing changing consumer demands for sustainable food supply. Startups like GoodBelly, Thryve and HUM are taking on nutrition, starting with our gut health. Habit, Viome, Nutrino and DayTwo are examples of companies addressing more personalized nutrition. Strava, ClassPass and others are creating ways for communities to get physically healthier, just as WellTok, Bravely and Wellbeats are working with employers to do the same through comprehensive health programmes for employees.

While most of these are focused on physical health and wellness, there are startups in nearly every industry that stay close to the needs of their communities, through technology and data-driven feedback. If we can improve both physical and mental health through these types of empathy-driven business models, we can also find startups focused on improving financial health. Here are some that stand out to us:

- **Chime**
  This is one of the startups that is doing things differently. It is a digital-only bank that is built on the principle of transparency – no hidden fees. Unlike most traditional banks, Chime does not

charge monthly fees and does not impose a minimum monthly balance requirement. It also offers a round-up feature that allows consumers to round up their purchase on the Chime debit card to the nearest dollar and deposit the difference into savings. As one of the 25 largest startups in the US and with a sizable customer base, Chime is showing that it can do well while doing good.

- **Pula**
  Another disruptive model, Pula is an insurtech startup that offers microinsurance to small farmers in Africa. Using satellite data to track rainfall, they provide replacement seeds for farmers to replant when the rain fails. With the bundling of insurance and farm inputs (eg seeds and fertilizer), this type of agriculture insurance product offers assistance to farmers when they need it and helps to maintain income stability at a time when livelihoods are increasingly being impacted by climate change.

- **Hello Tractor**
  The on-demand economy has been disrupting entertainment, transport and logistics businesses for the past decade; it was only a matter of time before it came to farming equipment. Hello Tractor was set up in partnership with John Deere. Under the programme, John Deere sells the equipment to contractors who rent it out to small farmers using the Hello Tractor platform. For the farmers, planting with a tractor provides better yields than planting by hand, which helps improve the food supply and drives sustainable food security in developing economies.

Nelson Mandela said that 'education is the most powerful weapon you can use to change the world.'[18] In today's world, we would add to that 'empathy', which provides us with the moral compass to look beyond ourselves. Equality feels like discrimination when you are used to privilege. By lifting those in need, we uplift our whole community. And together, we can all thrive in a stronger and better future. These are among the principles that drive us to go *Beyond Good*.

CHAPTER FIVE

Serving the forgotten

Only life lived for others is worthwhile.[1] ALBERT EINSTEIN

Serving one, serving all

Nothing reveals the inequality in the world more vividly than a crisis. More often than not, those who needed help the most before the crisis tend to be the most impacted. Over the past decade, we have witnessed a changing trend in how we work, fuelled by the adoption of smart devices that connect buyers and providers of various services. More corporations are moving towards the gig economy model, where they assign work on demand to a pool of contingent workers. Many have touted the flexibility of such a set-up, as more people can choose when, how and where they work. Such arrangements allow caregivers to earn a living when they are not taking care of their loved ones; it also enables older adults to perform part-time work post full-time employment. For many, this provides a much-needed secondary source of income. But at what cost? And as delivery services such as those provided by Uber Eats, Gojek and Deliveroo proliferate, who benefits the most? The disruptive technology provider that acts as the middleman? Or the low-wage essential worker?

More often than not the flexibility comes at the expense of the financial wellbeing of these gig workers, as many of these companies don't offer healthcare insurance, sick pay or retirement benefits. It's even more of a challenge when this is the primary source of income for these workers; if income is disrupted, as in the case of an economic downturn, gig workers are left on their own without any safety net. 'Should I pay rent? Or should I pay for my insurance?' become not hypothetical but real questions that workers need to grapple with. Although healthcare coverage being tied to work, as it is in the US, may not be the dominant issue for most contingent workers, putting healthy food on the table is surely common to their core concerns. Physical wellbeing takes a toll when financial wellbeing suffers. This is why there must be a different path as work becomes more transitory.

What could be done to better protect gig workers? And what about workers whose income often comes in other forms, for example, those working at startups where income streams are often constrained by equity external to standard pay cheques, or workers who are solo business owners? 'Let them eat cake,' certainly is not the answer. To find a solution, we will need to revisit the primary challenges of contingent work and the main concerns that keep these workers up at night:

- **Income volatility**
  Owing to the nature of the work, the income of gig workers is often unstable. Unfortunately, much of life's commitments often fall on a standard cycle: from rent and mortgages, from weekly food needs to utilities and childcare. The ability to

have a single view of all the income streams and provide tools to smooth out the income – enabling workers to save more on an upcycle to help cover the dips in income – is more important than ever. Startups such as Acorns, Steady and Stoovo are working on ways to help optimize income from multiple gig economy employers in this manner.

- **Lending**
  Without a stable income and employment contract, startup founders and gig workers face obstacles in obtaining financing from financial institutions. When faced with an income short-fall, they can easily fall prey to payday lenders, in order to gain quick access to liquidity. It is no wonder that superapps such as Grab and Gojek in Southeast Asia have started offering loans to their drivers, many of them microentrepreneurs without access to formal financial services. For solo entrepreneurs or workers at small startups, there need to be alternative ways of assessing credit risk and opportunities to assess ability to pay back loans as well.

- **Invoicing and tax support**
  Unlike regular full-time employment, taxes are not automatically withheld from the pay cheque for gig workers; many workers, especially those who are accustomed to a steady pay cheque in corporate jobs, often get surprised when tax filing season approaches. The ability to invoice, perform bookkeeping and file for taxes will save time and money for gig workers, as well as other workers who have inconsistent pay cheques.

- **On-demand microinsurance**
  Conventional insurance policies are typically issued on an annual basis. However, gig workers such as on-demand drivers and dog walkers, only need insurance coverage on a temporary basis, such as by the hour. More flexible business models are needed to offer insurance to those who work on a more contingent or less consistent basis.

- **Saving and investing**

  Beyond addressing their day-to-day financial needs, gig workers also need ways to save for the future. While many people opt for gig work to earn extra money for retirement, an increasing number of workers are full-time gig economy workers. According to a Betterment report,[2] 3 in 10 people who earn their primary income through the gig economy set aside no money for retirement regularly. Without the support of employer-sponsored retirement plans, they need access to services that can help them get started or stay on track. With solutions like Steady and Stoovo (both profiled in later chapters), the optimization of the financial needs of gig workers are finally starting to be addressed. As the nature of work changes, these solutions will become a new form of banking.

Despite the rise of contingency work, gig workers and small businesses, especially those in the West, remain underserved by most incumbent financial institutions. With availability of data and advanced analytics, however, we can change the narrative and support this growing workforce.

Look towards the East

Imagine the world we would have if we could just get out of our own way, create the type of broader ecosystems that could meet more than just our basic needs, shed our biases and close the gulf between what the world has become and what we know it should be. Nothing illustrates this better than the emergence of the technology titans inside China, where technology is reshaping the fundamental building blocks of the Chinese financial services ecosystem.

Small and medium-sized enterprises (SME) form the backbone of most economies, and China is no exception. As of February 2020, there were over 83.53 million individually owned businesses registered in China, employing more than 200 million people in total, according to China's State Administration for Market Regulation.[3] Over the past few years, small and medium-sized enterprises have contributed to more than 60 per cent of China's GDP and 80 per cent of urban employment. The importance of the deployment of digital finance as a tool to power these types of businesses cannot be understated. And China's two prominent tech giants, Alibaba and Tencent, have both made great strides to create ecosystems that enable these small enterprises to thrive. This harks back to what we said about sustainable business models in the last chapter.

Alipay, with over 1 billion users globally, is an online payment service launched in 2004, which has since evolved into the world's largest payment and lifestyle platform. At the centre of it all is an open technology platform, which allows Ant Group to collaborate with external parties.

MYbank, the online private commercial bank under Ant Group, for example, has served 29 million SMEs in China, including over 8.2 million women-operated businesses. Most notably, the majority of them (80 per cent) had never received business loans from a bank previously, and women-operated SMEs have a lower default risk compared to those operated by men, according to Ant Group's[4] data.

At the heart of this is Ant's open technology platform, heavily powered by artificial intelligence and cloud computing technologies. As part of MYbank's collateral-free business loans, for example, AI is used to determine interest rates and credit limits, which significantly helps to speed up the loan processing.

Alongside Ant Group is Tencent, whose superapp WeChat had, as of March 2020, over 1.2 million active users per month. Similar to MYbank is Tencent's WeBank, which focuses on the underbanked and SMEs, with over 200 million users spanning 600 cities. According to WeBank's 2019 annual report,[5] 75 per cent of the individual borrowers were blue-collar, and for 61 per cent of the SMEs this was the first time that they'd received a loan from a financial institution. According to the stats[6] published by Tencent, a total of 79.4 per cent of small to mid-sized merchants in China are WeChat Pay users, while WeChat has been identified as directly and indirectly creating 26.1 million job opportunities.

Similar stories are emerging in Southeast Asia, a region with 11 countries and over 655 million people. Just over a decade ago, four in five Southeast Asians had no internet connectivity and limited access to the internet. Today, Southeast Asians are the most engaged mobile internet users in the world, with 400 million internet users. Some 90 per cent of them connect to the internet primarily through their mobile phones, based on data from the e-Conomy SEA[7] research programme. The sum of digital payments is expected to exceed $1 trillion by 2025, accounting for almost one in every two dollars spent in the region.

Of the nearly 400 million adults in Southeast Asia, only 104 million are fully banked and enjoy full access to financial services; 98 million are underbanked, with a bank account but insufficient access to credit, investment and insurance; and 198 million remain unbanked – without a bank account. Similar to what we have described with China above, millions[8] of small and medium-sized enterprises face large funding gaps.

Gojek and Grab are two dominant players in the region. The former is Indonesia's first unicorn and the largest e-wallet in the country. It launched as a ride-hailing service in 2015, and has since expanded to cover a variety of on-demand services, as well as a cashless digital payments platform to address the needs of its microentrepreneurs. Similarly, Grab, another Southeast Asian unicorn, also started as a ride-hailing company in 2012. The superapp has since expanded into an array of digital services including transport, food delivery, mobile payments and insurance services, with 1.7 million microentrepreneurs reportedly opening their first bank account with Grab.

Myth-busting

Contrary to popular belief, not all gig economy workers are young adults. Many older adults seek contingency work as a secondary source of income or as a way to stay in the workforce and earn income post-retirement. And sadly, many will also face the reality of running out of savings in the later years of their lives as they live longer, out-spend limited public funds and face unexpected financial challenges.

As it turns out, the older population, rather like gig economy workers, is not well served by our existing financial services system. And many of the missed opportunities lie with the increased longevity of our general population.

Live longer, work longer?

On average, we are living an extra 30 years compared to the early 1900s. But how we live and how we work have changed dramatically with longevity. Not only are we leading healthier lifestyles, but we are also staying productive for longer. Some are working longer out of necessity (to earn extra income to sustain longevity); while others regard the extra time as a way to give back to the community.

According to the AARP Longevity Economy Outlook,[9] the 50-plus cohort in the US is composed of more than 117 million people, representing 35 per cent of the population across four generations. It is estimated that their economic contribution is equivalent to 40 per cent of the US economy's entire GDP. This cohort also plays a crucial role in supporting their aging parents, their children and grandchildren, as well as their communities through volunteering and charitable contributions, underpinning the social fabric of a country with almost 330 million people. In fact, every business sector stands to gain from the economic power of the aging cohort, from healthcare, transport, housing and leisure to financial services, clothing, education and technology. In particular, almost two-thirds of expenditure in the financial services and insurance industry is attributable to the 50-plus age group, according to the AARP report, so much so that in 2018, this demographic contributed nearly half the industry's GDP in the United States.

Around the world, the direct impact from consumption, wages and taxes creates a positive ripple effect on businesses and workers, generating income, consumption and production. Look no further than the number of purchases, online and offline, that grandparents make for their children and grandchildren. According to Pew Research Center,[10] a record 64 million Americans (one in five) live in multigenerational households. More people are now living long enough to see their great-grandchildren: by 2030, more than 70 per cent of the US 8-year-olds will have a living great-grandparent, according to Kenneth W Wachter,[11] Chairman of the Department of Demography at UC Berkeley.

Despite their economic power and contribution, the needs of this important demographic have been largely overlooked by various industries – much of it can be attributed to outdated bias against the aging population – that they are unproductive and a drain on society. But nothing could be further from the truth.

Changing the narrative

With the majority of children born in rich countries today expected to live past 100, multigenerational families – and a multigenerational workforce – will be more common. As we live longer and are no longer confined to retiring at 62 or 65, how we live, when we work or go back to school will also change. People are increasingly taking up entrepreneurship as a career choice, and more so later in life when they have gained work experience and have more financial flexibility. According to the *Harvard Business Review*,[12] the average age of a successful startup founder is 45. More businesses are also offering retraining and reskilling courses to help people adjust to new work environments.

Age is no longer a meaningful way to segment your customers; life stage matters more than the number of candles on our birthday cake. For financial institutions and beyond, this presents a golden opportunity to rethink how to serve the forgotten demographics – based on the stage of their lives and hence their needs, from asset accumulation to asset protection and decumulation.

For positive change to happen we need four things. The first is a focus on using human ingenuity to ensure that technology works to benefit us as humans, rather than a focus on removing humans from the production process. Secondly, we need to experiment. We do not yet know what works best so we need to start experimenting to find out. Thirdly, we need to create a social narrative that ensures an agenda set by all of us and not just corporates or governments. To do that will require finding ways to engage and build up civil society which needs to be at the heart of this social ingenuity, experimentation and new social narrative. ANDREW SCOTT, PROFESSOR OF ECONOMICS AT LONDON BUSINESS SCHOOL

One of the biggest concerns that people have when it comes to longevity is running out of money in later years. The questions 'How much should we save? And how much can we afford to spend on a daily basis?' might sound trivial – but being able to provide an answer is anything but.

To start with, financial institutions (or financial advisers) will need to understand one's financial obligations. With multigenerational households becoming more common, financial caregiving is likely to become a growing reality for many. Going forward, we will need better tools that can take into account multiple nodes (families), and we must not do it in a silo – for wealth and health go hand in hand. Having access to good healthcare and being able to live long and healthy lives will require financial resources. And the reverse is also true: poor health will impact not only longevity, but also the ability to accumulate wealth.

Financial exploitation of older adults

With more financial activities going digital, cybersecurity is becoming more challenging, especially when it comes to those who live alone or are not technologically savvy. Fraudsters prey on those who are lonely, since they will be more likely to talk to strangers for companionship – and over time, the victim may come to trust them enough to provide sensitive information (such as account ID and password), or even money. Scammers can also spoof or replicate the logos of trusted resources (such as a well-known bank) in emails or websites; consumers may unknowingly install malware on their computers that can allow it to scan their computers, or provide personal information, thinking that they are interacting with a legitimate website.

Financial fraud is not always committed by unknown strangers, however. Family members and friends can also be bad actors, with the elderly being particularly susceptible to financial exploitation, owing to the trust they place in people they know. According to the report 'Suspicious Activity Reports on Elder Financial Exploitation: Issues and Trends'[13] by the Consumer Financial Protection Bureau (CFPB), an agency of the US government, adults aged 70 to 79 suffered the highest average monetary loss ($45,300) to elder financial exploitation between 2013 and 2017. But that only represents the documented cases, which are likely to represent only a very small fraction of actual incidents, according to the CFPB. Moreover, monetary loss was more common and greater when the scammers were known to the elderly person (eg family members, fiduciaries or caregivers), compared to when they were strangers. Perhaps even more disturbingly, but unsurprisingly, the financial loss was greater when the scammers were fiduciaries.

Much more needs to be done to protect the financial security of older adults – and it will require collaboration between social services, law enforcement agencies, financial institutions and policymakers. We need more robust reporting from institutions and action by law enforcement agencies on suspicious activities. We need better intervention and prevention strategies; this can include blocking money transfer to suspicious accounts, leveraging technology to detect transaction patterns (eg a series of transfers to previously unassociated accounts) and provide timely alerts, and offering monitoring services for trusted family members or friends, who can help detect exploitation. Financial institutions can also set up different accounts for older adults (eg one with limited funds for caregivers), with different signature requirements.

Financial abuse of older adults is a multi-billion-dollar problem around the world, but the consequences go far beyond monetary loss. Many victims suffer from depression, which affects overall wellbeing. For those who have lost their life's savings and cannot recover the funds, they may need to adjust their lifestyle, or even forgo medication and other necessities, making it even more difficult to maintain their physical health.

Why aren't there more FinTech platforms focused on aging and financial health? Perhaps fraud monitoring isn't as sexy as robo-investors or blockchain ledgers. But given that older Americans control 83 per cent of US assets, providing families with tools that help protect their money presents a significant opportunity. FinTech can alert older people and caregivers about suspicious activity across financial accounts, credit cards, credit data and real estate in a way that exceeds what any one financial institution can do. I have seen firsthand the devastating fallout of elder financial abuse. It's time to disrupt the fraud-prevention systems that aren't working – and implement FinTech solutions that will truly make a difference. ELIZABETH LOEWY, CO-FOUNDER AND COO AT EVERSAFE

The future is multigenerational

While we are all aging, how we age is not homogeneous. And neither should our products and services be. Aside from protecting assets, we also need to consider a different way of financial planning when we think of long-term financial security. As mentioned earlier, we are living longer and leading more productive lives. We are more likely to work alongside multiple generations, and we are also more likely to be caring for multiple generations and households of loved ones. According to the Pew Research Center[14] analysis of US census data, a record 64 million people, or 20 per cent of the US population, lived with multiple generations under one roof in 2016.

To adequately address the needs of consumers and households, financial institutions need to create solutions that reflect how we live and interact as a society. While many caregivers of older adults are themselves getting older and will soon be needing care, more younger-generation family members are now picking up the burden of caregiving. According to AARP, a quarter of unpaid caregivers are millennials, and a *typical* caregiver is a 49-year-old woman. As many of these caregivers are still employed and likely to have a family of their own, how do they juggle work and caring for their loved ones? And more importantly, do they have the right tools that allow them to financially plan for multiple households?

Many of these caregivers are thrust into caregiving triggered by a crisis (eg a fall or a stroke). As much as it is a biological norm to get older, we don't have a timeline for when we need care. Unlike giving birth, for example, where you have a somewhat predictable timeline, along with a team of medical professionals and a playbook of sorts, caring for older adults is much more challenging. No two scenarios are exactly alike, making planning more difficult. It is not surprising that caregivers are often stressed – mentally, physically and financially.

What if we can provide a means for family members to save in advance for caregiving, in the same way that we encourage parents to save for their children's education? For example, in the US, many companies have employer-sponsored 401k plans to help their employees save for retirement, and each state has 529 plans to encourage parents to save for their children's higher education. The idea of introducing something similar to help caregivers save for caregiving expenses for their loved ones, in a tax-advantaged scenario, shouldn't seem that far-fetched, especially in a country where people aged 60 and above bear the biggest increase of student loan debt from 2010 to 2017, according to TransUnion.[15]

What if we changed the way in which we offered financial services – if, instead of pushing individual products, we offered a different dimension of planning and managing money for multiple households? This illustrates, yet again, the pressing need for us to shift from traditional product segmentation by age to that by life stage. It is time to shed our biases and presumptions about aging and confront our outdated stereotypes.

As Paul Irving, Chairman of the Milken Institute Center for the Future of Aging, noted in his brilliant report, 'Silver to Gold: The business of aging',[16] 'The new longevity frontier is more than a cache of years tacked on at the end of life: it is an integral part of life's continuum. The answer is not age segregation, but recognition of shared interests across generations.'

Financial planning isn't just for the privileged

One crucial question remains: when will I run out of money if I retire now? As mentioned earlier, this is a seemingly simple question that is anything but. Much of it is dependent on the economic condition, one's financial obligations (not only one's own obligations but also towards others, as in the caregiving discussions mentioned above), as well as health. As we stay in the workforce longer, likely with multiple income sources (for example, from gig work or our own ventures), trying to figure out our tax obligations, how much we need to save and how much we can afford to spend is becoming more complex.

While much of the financial services innovation focuses on asset accumulation, we cannot lose sight of the growing importance of asset decumulation. Consumers need help navigating the increasing complexities of financial planning and understanding where the trade-offs are. While high-net-worth individuals can rely on the services of paid financial advisers, advances in artificial intelligence and advanced data analytics might offer a more cost-efficient way for us to broaden access to those who truly need the help.

Along with expanding financial management, financial institutions can also help their customers better understand and access government benefits that they might be eligible for. Many such tools are available online, but they can be incredibly complex to navigate. Having the financial institution (perhaps someone at the branch or a trusted partner) be part of the process can prove to be beneficial to older adults, so that they can access some much needed funds; and it will further cement the trust and relationship between the older adult and the financial institution.

Supporting age-friendly banking goes beyond having big fonts. If we take a more in-depth look at how people are living and where their needs truly are we can create a more inclusive system that serves a broader community.

Purpose... is about reaching out, getting involved and acting on those instincts and inclinations to add value for others and meaning to life. If what we are going through doesn't change us and call us to action, what will? PAUL IRVING, CHAIRMAN OF THE CENTER FOR THE FUTURE OF AGING AT THE MILKEN INSTITUTE

SPOTLIGHT ON PAUL IRVING AND THE MILKEN INSTITUTE CENTER FOR THE FUTURE OF AGING

Even as AI and machine learning outstrip human capabilities – as coding becomes a robotic function – people will continue to bring wisdom and humanity to the table. The human soul is not replaceable.

Those were the very words from Paul Irving, Chairman of the Milken Institute Center for the Future of Aging, whose mission is to 'improve lives and strengthen societies by promoting healthy, productive and purposeful aging'. The Center is part of the Milken Institute, a non-profit, non-partisan think tank founded in 1991 by Mike Milken to advance prosperity across the globe.

And as the chairman of Encore.org, an organization that promotes intergenerational solutions to challenging social problems, Paul has long advocated strategies that reintegrate the generations together, from academia to housing and the workplace, as a vehicle to bridge new skills and develop fresh approaches. 'Age segregation is unnatural', as Paul likes to say.

By 2024, one in four US workers will be aged 55-plus. By 2030, there will be more people over the age of 60 worldwide than there will be under the age of 10.[17] Aging is something that we all have in common; and we should all have an interest in making older life more fulfilling and purposeful, not just for ourselves, but also for our children and grandchildren. And as Paul stresses, we must recognize that everyone has something to contribute, especially in our later years. Yet, this experience of aging is not always a time when we can all contribute equally, and for some it represents some of life's darker moments. Some will face financial poverty in old age, even homelessness. In fact, people aged 50 and over now comprise approximately one-third of homeless Americans. If the attitudes from the recent pandemic are anything to go by, where the lives of older adults are being perceived as expendable, our society is failing the moral test miserably.

Celebrating longevity involves a cultural shift. We need educators and communicators; we need to change the view of employers on work life; and we need to create new retirement norms. But above all, we need to value the lives and experience of the older adults among us. Every age and stage of our lives brings something new; we just need an opportunity to realize the possibilities.

While we are at it, as Paul notes, let's create a better future for the generations to come. That is a legacy we can all be proud of.

The moral test of any society is how it treats its most vulnerable members, including those who are old and living in the shadows. PAUL IRVING, CHAIRMAN OF THE CENTER FOR THE FUTURE OF AGING AT THE MILKEN INSTITUTE

Opportunities hiding in plain sight

While we have seen an increased representation of women in the boardroom and executive teams, the uptake has been slow and varies widely across culture and industries, according to the CS Gender 3000 Report[18] by Credit Suisse. Roles held by women remain clustered away from operational decision-making – a factor that impacts the chances of women being promoted to chief executive. And the road to equality remains uneven. In the US, for example, according to the Equal Pay Day Report[19] from organization Women Who Code, in Silicon Valley the average man earns 61 per cent more than the average woman. And that figure varies by marginalized group: for every dollar that white, non-Hispanic men earn, Black women are paid 61 cents, compared to Latina women at 53 cents and Asian women at 85 cents.

These injustices – the racial wage gap and lack of fair and equitable access to credit, the housing-ownership gap and college-degree-attainment gap – are not accidental. Rather, they are the result of long-standing systemic racial and social discrimination. And it comes at a cost: According to Citi's 'Closing the Racial Inequality Gap Report',[20] 'If racial gaps for Blacks had been closed 20 years ago, US GDP could have benefited by an estimated $16 trillion.'

Economic equality is a human right.
SCOTT ASTRADA, ADJUNCT PROFESSOR OF LAW AT GEORGETOWN UNIVERSITY CENTER AND DIGITAL CIVIL SOCIETY FELLOW, STANFORD UNIVERSITY, CENTER ON PHILANTHROPY AND CIVIL SOCIETY

To be successful, we need to mirror the diversity of the communities we serve. Having different voices from different backgrounds provides us with different perspectives when examining problems at hand, enabling us to be more innovative and thoughtful in the solutions that we offer. Numerous studies have shown that diversity drives positive business results. But how do we get there?

Balancing career and family

While it has become increasingly socially normal for women to have a career and family at the same time, women still predominantly perform much of the domestic housework. According to Melinda Gates, women spend seven more years on average performing household work than men. The extra time spent doing unpaid housework and taking care of children takes away the time that women can use to socialize with others or learn something new to further their education or career. While caregiving can be meaningful, sharing the responsibility would be beneficial not only for women, but also for the wellbeing of the children, as they would have more opportunities to bond with both parents.

To achieve meaningful changes, we will need the help of all members of society, because attaining gender diversity is not just a women's issue, it is a societal challenge. One great example of this is paternity leave. In Nordic countries where parental leave is generous, it is not uncommon for both fathers and mothers to take an extended period of time off to tend to their newborn. Sweden, for example, offers 240 days of parental leave for each parent after a baby's birth. Not only are both parents encouraged to take the paid time off, the days do not expire until the child is eight years old. Having such a system in place not only encourages fathers to take an active role in parenting, it also reduces the stigma around parental leave. A further plus is that 'parental' or 'family' leave is a more gender-neutral description than 'maternity leave'.

Another important factor in the equation is affordable childcare, which encourages parents to return to work after taking parental leave. Conversely, when childcare is expensive, one of the parents will likely opt to stay in full-time parenting or switch to lower paid but more flexible part-time work. And in many scenarios, women are the ones who take the step back with their career, and return only after the children are older. Not only does this impact the immediate economic wellbeing of women owing to diminished potential earning power, but it also negatively affects their long-term financial security, leaving them with less accumulated wealth.

Diversity and inclusion at work

Gender diversity is not just a pipeline challenge. We must have an inclusive culture in order to retain the women who join the workforce, so they don't feel isolated in the boys' club. Having an inclusive environment dictates that all voices are heard and that each employee of the company feels valued and respected. They are encouraged to speak up and voice their opinion, regardless of their background, and managers are held accountable for ensuring diversity in their teams.

While networking outside of the office is a great way to encourage communication and collaboration between teams, it is important to consider the needs of working parents, who often have to attend extracurricular activities with their school-aged children. As many decisions are often made outside of the four walls of the corporate environment, being inclusive and considerate in ensuring working parents, especially women, have access to those opportunities is crucial. One cannot overlook the serendipitous moments that such networking events can bring about.

Have you ever noticed the gender of the people who are more prominently featured in financial services advertising, and how the media-reporting differs when it comes to women leaders versus men? Or the age of consumers who are typically targeted for FinTech apps? How about the ethnicity of startup founders participating in pitch competitions?

Diversity and inclusion are important not only for large organizations, but also businesses of all sizes. And diversity extends beyond gender; to be truly inclusive, we must embrace diversity of thought, age, socio-economic background, education, sexual orientation and ethnicity.

Unfortunately, despite increased awareness and scrutiny, our corporate world and our innovation ecosystem remain stubbornly homogeneous. We all know the numbers and they are dismal. According to Catalyst,[21] 'Women of color hold just 4.6 per cent of board seats in the Fortune 500. Yet they represent approximately 18 per cent of the US population.' Even though female founders received a record $3.54 billion in funding in 2019, this represented only 2.7 per cent of the total venture capital investments, according to PitchBook data. As a point of comparison, WeWork garnered more investment than all global female founders combined in 2019. Irony aside, the missed opportunity makes one despair.

Now, imagine our disappointment when the news came that venture funding for female founders in the third quarter of 2020 has hit a three-year low, reverting back to the 2017 level, despite the overall investments being on par with previous years.[22]

While talent is equally distributed, opportunity is not. We must act urgently to change the narrative, so that the innovation economy can serve the greater good for all in society. We must make entrepreneurship more inclusive by extending opportunities to diverse minds and talents in all corners of society, regardless of age, ethnicity, background and gender.

SPOTLIGHT ON VILLAGE CAPITAL

Village Capital is a global accelerator that supports impact-driven, seed-stage startups, along with an affiliated fund, VilCap Investments. Village Capital has supported companies in 28 countries; 46 per cent of their portfolio companies are founded by women and 30 per cent are Black or Latinx. Both of these figures are much higher than the industry average.[23]

They are also unique in their areas of focus: Sustainability, Financial Health and the Future of Work, all of which are sectors that directly impact the financial wellbeing of consumers and small businesses, as well as the long-term viability of our civilization as a whole. Some of their portfolio companies include:

- **Landit**
  A technology platform designed to increase the engagement and success of women and diverse groups in the workplace and help companies attract a diverse workforce. It has a presence in over 20 countries (and counting).

- **MPOWER Financing**
  A public benefit corporation that extends credit to international students based on their potential, rather than the traditional model, which requires an established US credit history, collateral or a cosigner.

- **Vault**
  Previously called Student Loan Genius, Vault enables companies to make student loan repayment an employee benefit. It allows employers to use the matching funds they would otherwise contribute to their employee's 401k plans to go towards student loan payments.

- **PiggyVest**
  The first and largest online savings and investing platform in Nigeria, enabling savers to put away funds that they don't want to withdraw easily. By restricting access, it helps its users maintain their savings discipline while building their savings habit.

The impact results thus far have been inspiring. Here are some of the metrics proving that point:

- 144.2 million pounds of CO_2 emissions offset;
- 27.5 million low-income students served;
- 1.6 million low-income patients reached;
- 652,000 people provided with access to affordable financial services;
- 15,200 smallholder farmers served;
- 13,400 jobs created.

For those who argue against the business case for diversity in entrepreneurship, perhaps there is really another way after all. And Village Capital is showing us how.

There is so much data out there now that shows that economic performance suffers if you don't have diversity on your team. It is only reasonable that you want to back diverse teams from the start. VICTORIA FRAM, VILCAP INVESTMENTS

SPOTLIGHT ON SPRINGBOARD

Springboard is a global accelerator based in Washington DC, whose mission is to accelerate the growth of entrepreneurial companies led by women through access to essential resources and a global community of experts. Its accelerator programmes focus on enterprise solutions, spanning digital health, life science, technology and fashion tech.

True to its collaborative roots, Springboard offers entrepreneurs actionable insights and resources from knowledgeable people in the community through their signature Dolphin Tanks. With 800 companies having presented in 150 Dolphin Tank sessions across 42 cities in 14 countries, Amy Millman, President and Co-Founder of Springboard, often stresses: 'It's not about sharks or piranhas but rather, "How can we help?"'

According to metrics provided by the accelerator, since 2000, over 800 Springboard portfolio companies, seeking financial and human capital for product development and expansion, have created over $22.5 billion in value, are revenue generators and job creators. Numbers do speak louder than words.

Entrepreneurs are sheroes. AMY MILLMAN, PRESIDENT AND CO-FOUNDER, SPRINGBOARD ENTERPRISES

SPOTLIGHT ON SUNRISE BANKS

Having looked at renewed business models in the previous chapter and serving forgotten demographics in the current, it's time to discuss the spectre of profit within financial services. Can banking's business model better serve their communities by focusing on the financial health of the people in them? We would like to introduce you to a special organization that shows you that you can do just that.

Sunrise Banks, a certified B Corporation headquartered in St Paul, Minnesota, is a certified CDFI (Community Development Financial Institution) and is a member of the GABV (the Global Alliance for Banking on Values). GABV is an independent network of 62 financial institutions using finance to deliver sustainable economic, social and environmental development. Sunrise Banks focuses on financially inclusive products and financial education that especially helps lower-income customers improve their financial lives. The bank also gives back a minimum of 2 per cent net income per year to their community through corporate donations and sponsorships. In 2019, the bank was named best in the world by B Lab for the seventh consecutive year.[24] Sunrise Banks truly embraces inclusive business practices and is a role model for other financial institutions:

- 58 per cent of their employee demographics are female and 30 per cent are minority.
- 29 per cent of their employees live in low-to-moderate-income (LMI) communities.

Profits and purpose can – and should – co-exist. The story of Sunrise Banks, relayed by their CEO, David Reiling, is a true testament to how our society can become, from banking industry and beyond.

'I bought a bank with my dad 25 years ago. The purchase didn't look good on paper. The bank had $14 million in total assets on a good day; it was located in a neighborhood with the highest rate of 911 calls in the city; and faced persistent regulatory problems, specifically for redlining, the act of denying loans to a specific group of people. Oftentimes poor people of colour were affected most.

'But from the outset, I was confident I could turn things around on one premise: the only way the bank was going to succeed was if the community succeeded. My immigrant Italian grandmother lived in this neighborhood and I spent a lot of time with her growing up. I understood our immigrant neighbours and used this advantage to seek innovative solutions that provided this community with access to convenient, easy-to-use and fairly priced financial services.

'Today, a quarter of a century later, we've proven that our "doing well by doing good" model is not just effective, but scalable. By creating a mission-driven institution that stood up for its community – its residents and businesses – Sunrise was able to effectively improve and grow its neighborhood businesses and households while maintaining a safe and sound regulated financial institution. In short, we demonstrated that you can indeed "do well by doing good."

'Sunrise Banks has grown to $1.4 billion in assets since its inception, achieving 10 times growth. At the same time, we've also achieved exceptional growth in the positive impact we create for the people and communities we serve. Sunrise's place-based mission focus was the innovation sandbox that propelled it to create impact at scale via payment and FinTech partnerships nationally.

'Sunrise is a certified B Corp with a score of 142. This score ranked us in the top 10 per cent of B Corps (in any industry) worldwide for the seventh consecutive year in 2019. This is not to boast (we Minnesotans aren't good at that sort of thing), but to have you understand that competing to be the "Best for the World" is where we lean in and take a stand. It's about being the best *for* the world, not *in* the world. We want to be a leader among the world's B Corps. Each year we have to strive to be better so we can continue to help the people that we serve to succeed.

'Talk is cheap. As a US Treasury Certified Community Development Financial Institution (CDFI), Sunrise has originated at least 60 per cent of its loans in low-to-moderate income census tracts each year since 2001. This commitment to serving those places and people generally left out by traditional financial institutions speaks to Sunrise's core value of working for something "Bigger Than Us". It is a blessing to receive a double pay cheque – monetary compensation that supports your family and an emotional pay cheque that supports your purpose.

'Mission is good business. We call it mission times margin (mission x margin). This is the abundance mindset: the more intentional you are about "doing good" the easier it is to "do well". I believe that if businesses want to go "Beyond Good" they have to leave behind the scarcity mindset, the idea that mission subtracts from margin. Moreover, they have to see their mission as an integral part of their business instead of a supplemental component that's "nice to have".

'Companies that go beyond good usually have servant leaders at the helm. These servant leaders are not afraid to stand for something; they believe and act with intentionality because it is authentic to them to "be good" and actually do good. You can't be a wimp if you want to lead a mission-driven company. You are charged with making decisions that live in the grey. It's easy to make black-and-white decisions about maximizing shareholder value. It's hard to balance the interest of all stakeholders.

'While we strive to be our best, mission-driven self, we cannot do this alone. We collaborate and partner with others to share risk, rewards, insights and ideas. At Sunrise, we're often invisible to the end user of our product or service. The people we want to help trust our front-stage partners more than they would a financial institution. Simply said, some people just don't trust banks. Our organizational ego takes a backseat to executing our mission for the benefit of others.

'The economic disparities in this country are dire, and they've been made worse by the Covid-19 pandemic. The coronavirus pandemic has disproportionately affected minority groups both economically and in terms of physical health. The widespread inequity among racial and ethnic groups was again made painfully obvious during the summer of 2020 when George Floyd was killed by Minneapolis Police.

'Our country is in desperate need of a paradigm shift that prioritizes everyone's physical, emotional and economic wellbeing, no matter their background. And Sunrise Banks has been working to effect this necessary change since our beginning. It hasn't always been easy, and it definitely hasn't always been popular. But it's what we believe in.

'Today, Sunrise Banks might seem like an anomaly. We're a for-profit company – a bank, no less – that's proven we can do well by doing good. But change is coming at revolutionary speed. I see it in Sunrise staff and my children every day. Good is moving at exponential speed; this is just the beginning.

'It was 50 years ago that Milton Friedman claimed that a corporation's sole responsibility was to increase its profits for shareholders. Half a century later that maxim is seen as a dated and myopic view of corporations and their role in society. If 2020 is any indication of how much change we will witness in the next decade, now is the time to go beyond good. The sooner we make the transition, the better off we'll be.'

A way forward

Financial services seem to lack a true north in regard to acting as fiduciary for every customer at scale, and startups are quickly acting to exploit this. Customers with lingering distrust around traditional banking have become more likely to abandon it for FinTech solutions. This has started to change the way banks invest, partner and build both customer-facing and back-office technologies. Banks need to embrace changes beyond those that drive efficiencies and short-term profitability. To truly become agents of a more progressive model, banking itself needs a reset.

What if banking doesn't change? The likely answer is disruption, in the form of external technology providers that better serve customers at scale. During the past decade, Amazon has grown from selling books online to disrupting everything from cloud computing to grocery shopping. Facebook has grown to connect a third of the global population while becoming one of the largest ad platforms ever created. Google and Apple have redefined categories and impacted customer relationships in every vertical. Chinese e-commerce platforms created by technology companies such as Ant Group and Tencent have demonstrated innovation within massive open frameworks.

As these digital platforms have arisen, the initial moves by these tech giants into banking services – most notably payments and credit – may soon alter the perception of what a successful financial enterprise looks like. The way financial brands embrace the rise in the scale and pace of their challengers is critical. What we do for our community, our employees and our customers speaks volumes about our values, more than empty words promised during annual shareholder meetings or on the hillside of Davos. Where we put our investment dollars matters.

It is not beyond our ability to serve the needs of everyone in society. We only lack the will. And that too seems to be changing towards the arc of the common good. How creative banks are in building new forms of customer value – and increasingly more inclusive means of serving their communities – may determine their very survival.

Beyond Good in the end is a story about business models that puts purpose and community above scale and profits, and those models that can achieve both to assure a more equal future for all. We must listen to more voices and answer their call of need.

CHAPTER SIX

The profit conundrum

It is dreams that drive the world, not just the technology.[1] JACK MA, ALIBABA

Welcome to the machine

When we enter the workforce of billions, we are joining an ancient machine of collective human endeavour. Regardless of which profession we choose – or have chosen for us by the fate and circumstances of where and to whom we were born – these choices impact our orientation within society. Our work comes to define much of who we are, shaping our experiences, our values and our beliefs, as well as our personal paths. As part of humanity's diverse labour force, the vast majority of us exchange our productivity for wages as we become part of a machine that helps fulfil the collective needs of our global community. We work, we receive income, we exchange that for the products of the labour of others (to fulfil both wants and needs). Others receive income in exchange and subsequently buy their own goods and services – this is the global market economy at work. Seeing the cycle of our labour as part of this system of connected activities – seeing that forest through those trees – is a fundamental requirement for the optimization of our labour towards the arc of the common good.

It is through the effort of work that we receive personal profit, but this is where the compensation that we receive for our labour and the profit that a business receives for its output may diverge. Where we work, what we produce, the impact that our product has on others – do these align with our values? Does what we do improve the lives of our family and others? Does it make our community a better place to live? These are questions we must ask ourselves, as the spectre of profit is present in most of our endeavours. Does what we do (and why) match up to the story we told ourselves when we started working where we work (if we had any choice in the matter, that is)? Are we working at a company, or in an industry, or in the service of others, that improves society? Does the profit of our work have a positive or negative impact on society? Can we afford to think of the role of our work this way? The economic reality that we've painted thus far is one of inequality for much of humanity – and one with few choices: just keep my family fed and keep a roof over our head, please. For those with greater work mobility there is a choice; one that matters. For most of the workforce there are fewer choices devolving to a more desperate state.

Self-employed workers and small-business owners help set both rates in the market for their services and the direction of their labour. They help define the purpose of their business, and work to optimize a target level of personal profit. For the majority of workers, however, and increasingly for those tied to the gig economy, wages and employment status are less in their direct control – these workers do not generally have a voice in the choices that the company makes, the level of profit, the fluctuation of its worth, inventory and balance sheets. They only know that if they drive for longer hours, deliver more food and packages, and work longer, they can earn more income. But who pays for their employee benefits in those societies that do not cover important basic needs like healthcare? And what happens when they fall ill and cannot work? Who is there to help these workers better understand the impact of their labour on their financial lives and of the opportunities presented to the generation after them? Outside of economists, politicians, unions and think tanks, who advocates for the interests of those on the bottom of the pyramid of wages and wealth? Something has to change, as we are all part of this invisible hand, part of a collective force that can help shape a more equal society.

In most business models, the workers on the front line are often given the least consideration when it comes to distributing the profit of their shared labour. In large corporations, jobs are often the first to be cast aside at any hint of economic downturn or when there is a need to boost stock prices or valuation. The continued development of technology that improves the efficiency of labour – to the extent of replacing physical workers themselves – has significant consequences. The reality is that fewer and fewer people have choices about where they work and what they do, how productive they can be, how much they earn, and how much they can afford with the fruits of their labour. This alone has an impact on the growing inequality – often unseen – within our communities. We must be more cognizant of how our choices intersect with both the greater economic system and with each other. Everything is connected to everything else in the end.

How much then should any individual, family, company or industry truly profit? You might say that it is left up to the markets, to the economics of supply and demand, to the application of technology and skills and effort (or, in many cases, luck). But there's more to it than that. Would we see such disparate income and wealth stratification if the foundation of these profits were truly scrutinized by society? Would we see such broad inequality if public policy matched political rhetoric? Questioning the appropriate level of profit and wealth creation becomes this conundrum – a question somewhat difficult to answer save by those who gain the most from it. Isn't there another way?

Consider the following from Credit Suisse's 2019 Global Wealth Report: the bottom half of adults globally accounted for less than 1 per cent of total global wealth, while the richest top 10 per cent possessed 82 per cent of global wealth and the top 1 per cent alone owns nearly half (45 per cent) of all assets.[2] This inverted wealth pyramid reflects the disparity of income and associated wealth derived from wages versus those created through investments, inherited wealth and entrepreneurial endeavours leveraging external sources of capital.

The distribution of the profit of a society should matter to everyone, as it impacts both our standard of living and reflects our societal standards of fairness. As we continue to present the ideas around sustainable equality within our communities, think about your own lives and how money has impacted your family and the life you have been able to lead. It is important that we check our privilege, question our own biases and challenge the existing paradigm in order to consider our lot in life compared to the rest of the global community.

The era of materiality, though not yet over, seems to be finding a new balance with social consciousness – that encompasses inclusiveness, diversity and sustainability. Wholistic living is emerging to be the new aspiration. The current economic and technical environment has drastically shortened the typical company life cycle. The only way ahead for businesses is to evolve towards the same social consciousness. Those who do will be respected and eventually last longer, though their journey to profitability may be longer. NIDHI PRABHU, FINTECH AND DIGITAL STRATEGY CONSULTANT

The economics of the common good

What mechanisms do we have for considering the fairness of a society? Economics as a social science studies the production, consumption and distribution of goods and services. While much of what you see in the news focuses on the macroeconomic view of the economy – concentrating on the public and private levers that can be used to control the allocation of finite resources and to steer the economy towards a specific outcome – we must pay equal attention to the plight of individuals, households and businesses, and connect them to the fair distribution of social wealth. We need more focus on the ethical dilemmas beyond the data – on the fact that the opportunity cost around macroeconomic choices has long-lasting implications for the microeconomics of human lives. Understanding the context of profit may be the key to change, but genuine empathy remains the driver.

> *The FinTech industry has as many sub-sectors and purposes as there are participants. I believe though firmly that the ultimate legacy of the innovations and the changes that come from FinTech will be to help the less privileged among us to live a better – financial – life. We should never forget that humankind always depends on change and innovation to survive. We are only strong together, and it is our responsibility to help the less fortunate to live a better life. We win as a team.* SPIROS MARGARIS, MARGARIS VENTURES

The concepts within economic theory – the analysis of competition, complexity, ignorance, imperfection, inequality, scarcity, subjectivity and others – must continue to take into consideration how much more connected our global society has become. And we must, as more informed consumers and more empathetic leaders, be equally thoughtful about how our decisions affect the other 7.5 billion people in the world. Every decision we make as global citizens truly matters. As leaders, every decision we make or influence matters – from the smallest action to the broadest policy.

How we leverage the drivers within our economy matters. While technology has increasingly become the catalyst for creating more of what everyone needs (food, water and shelter), we still have many ways to improve. Although we have increased yields of necessary staple crops such as corn, rice and wheat over the past decades and improved access to clean water, there remains a growing inequality around income and wealth across most societies. While many in the West see their wants increasingly fulfilled by the algorithms of large technology firms, there are still many swathes of the population in developed nations that do not have their basic needs met. This is the conundrum of profit-sharing within a society: even as there is growing wealth, there is growing inequity. At the heart of this are human decisions. We cannot change society towards the arc of the common good if leaders aren't willing to empathize and act.

Our increasingly technology-enabled world has shifted the output of physical labour towards a global economy that benefits fewer and fewer people, derived from a focus around business output that is less tangible, less able to support the basic needs of 7.5 billion people. More importantly, with growing inequality in society, the metrics that we once relied on no longer fully reflect the complexity and nuances of our global economy. A question that leaders must ask themselves today is whether we measure the success of an economy solely by its growth or rather by who truly benefits from that growth?

At its core, economics is fundamentally about relationships between people, the communities we live in and society as a whole. It is about choices we make both personally, professionally and as a society. The type of economic condition we are born into may not necessarily be a choice we would have made, but the economy we create is one of the choices thrust upon us.

The cadence of economic discussion needs to be more in tune with the reality beyond the ivory towers of universities. To make the theories of economics more accessible, it is important to understand that economic decisions – both small and large – are made by people in the end, not institutions. Yet the structure of institutions is why decisions are made the way they are. The behaviour of individuals within institutions is shaped by the realities of their own lives – often very different from those who are impacted by them. What gets produced, who gets what, who has to make it, who gets to consume it, and who makes money from it – these are important questions that should make us think differently about the economics of our communities. In that, there is some hope.

A new generation of economists, such as Heather Boushey of the Washington Center for Equitable Growth, has argued that extreme inequality limits our economic potential, and advocates bold rethinking of our economic policies. The economy, as we know it, is not working for everyone. In her book, *Unbound: How inequality constricts our economy and what we can do about it*,[3] she rejects the presumption that 'a rising tide lifts all boats'. It is not enough to just know how much the economy has grown, but also how much incomes have grown for those in different brackets of income distribution. We must focus on new ways to give more parts of society a leg up.

While the last century saw much success in reducing the number of people living in extreme poverty, the global income and subsequent wealth gap has only grown. Wealth is concentrated in the hands of a very few; individuals owning over $100,000 in assets make up less than 11 per cent of the global population yet control 82.8 per cent of global wealth.[4] In the paper, 'Vision 2020: Evidence for a stronger economy', referring to the divergence between the average and actual fortunes of families, Boushey said: 'This divergence makes GDP increasingly misleading as a guide to public policy: It does little good to target GDP as an outcome if the majority of GDP growth flows to a small group of families, leaving the rest with few gains.'[5]

We need new metrics to guide our economic policies – to truly reflect the complexities of our modern-day society and allow everyone in our economy to prosper. We must move beyond the notion that a rising gross domestic product (GDP) is the best way to measure the wealth of nations; that a rising stock market equates to a strengthening middle class, and that simply providing access to payments means broader financial inclusion for the poor. A broader measure of economic performance, the Inclusive Development Index (IDI), created by the World Economic Forum, bases wealth on the wider society and 'their household's standard of living – a multidimensional phenomenon that encompasses income, employment opportunity, economic security and quality of life.'[6]

The old adage says that we can't improve what we don't measure. We would suggest that you can't create a society focused on creating the greater good of each community if our measurements of success do not provide a place for every person to sit at the table of our collective prosperity.

Across the globe, we have made remarkable progress in bringing people into the formal financial system, but that has not necessarily translated into better economic outcomes – that is the industry's next challenge. TILMAN EHRBECK, MANAGING PARTNER AT FLOURISH VENTURES

SPOTLIGHT ON FLOURISH VENTURES

Flourish Ventures is a venture firm that began as part of Omidyar Network. The team invests in early-stage startups around the world, which help low-to-middle-income households and small businesses achieve financial wellbeing and prosperity. It was spun out in 2019 as an evergreen fund, with $300 million in capital along with its original portfolio of companies.

The firm makes impact-oriented investments in multiple sectors, including challenger banks, personal finance, insurtech, regtech and other technologies that empower people and enable a more inclusive economy. For example, Aspiration and Chime are both mobile-first digital-only challenger banks that offer unique products and business models built on transparency and trust; Propel leverages technology to help low-income Americans better manage their social safety-net benefits; Steady focuses on opportunities for gig economy workers, a growing demographic underserved by traditional financial institutions; Pula, an insurtech based in Kenya, uses technology to help smallholder farmers endure climate risks and enable them to invest more in their farm.

True to their mission, Flourish Ventures' steadfast focus on creating a fairer financial-services ecosystem to empower everyday consumers and small businesses is guided by their Fair Finance principles:

- Financial services empower people to achieve their life goals.
- Business models are built on consumer trust and business trustworthiness.
- People have meaningful control over how their financial data is collected and used.
- The financial infrastructure is open, low-cost and drives competitive markets.
- Digitally native regulation protects consumers and promotes innovation.

As the team at Flourish demonstrates, a company can be financially sustainable while helping consumers and small businesses attain positive financial outcomes. Purpose and profit, as it turns out, can co-exist in the real world.

The purpose of profit

The capitalist economic system centres on private ownership of profit – the financial gain between what was earned and what was spent in order to create some form of value. But what is the purpose of profit, when some industries and populations gain more than others, often to the detriment of the common good? Earlier, when we discussed Jim Collins's *Good to Great*, the focus of the truly great companies he profiled was on maximizing profit and creating shareholder value – one that echoes the sentiments of both Milton Friedman and Adam Smith (the latter of which called economics 'the *science of wealth*'). Yet there is an increasing development of more sustainable business models and broader definitions of corporate social responsibility (CSR) – one that adds transparency on how businesses accommodate shareholders (those that own equity or long-term forms of company value) versus how they support stakeholders (those individuals, entities and communities impacted by the business's actions, products and level of profit).

This movement towards more inclusive, community-minded, sustainable business models has gained momentum in the past decades. But what impact will it have if we don't change mindsets and cultural attitudes about profitability and its social impact on more of the world? Or debate policy changes around how levels of personal and corporate profit impact society – related to taxation and funding public infrastructure – or how best to regulate products that may harm the long-term health and financial wellbeing of our communities? How do we institutionalize empathy? We need to rethink how we can bend the business model towards the stakeholder model, one that considers the needs of every voice in the community that a business serves. This starts with education – at the very earliest age.

What if we put inequality and inclusion at the heart of our curriculum, and provided students more context to what they were learning as it relates to the real world around them? Our sense of fairness, our ability to empathize with others with differing levels of income and opportunity, our understanding of how much others in our global society have and have not – about how profit translates to an individual's income and perceived value – these are concepts and biases we develop from an early age. We may wonder why teachers and nurses aren't paid more than people who play professional sports or run hedge funds. We may struggle to understand why people of different races and cultures and incomes often live in different areas of a single city, not being aware that long-standing exclusive policies shaped such formations. We may not understand how money is created and distributed, how companies are created and how they evolve. If we were to understand more about how profit translates to an individual's income and what this means over time, then perhaps we wouldn't have the need to continually update our business ethics education (we will address this more in a later chapter).

How did we conclude that profit must come with a zero-sum game – that someone's profit must be another group's loss? Do we question why a CEO's compensation is 320 times as much as that of a typical worker, reflecting an increase of 105.1 per cent from 2009 to 2019 (compared to 7.6 per cent for the average worker over the same period),[7] or why certain executives fly on private jets when pensions aren't fully funded? These aren't debates about who takes on more risk; these aren't debates about qualifications of leaders; these aren't even necessarily debates about fairness. The pursuit of profit often pits one class against another, places one part of society a rung above the lower. And yet we don't discuss this enough; it is rarely debated by those who have control of a business's profit and the majority who do not. Thankfully, this is changing, as more shareholders are demanding greater transparency.

The output of every profession impacts our community. Whether you achieve certain levels of primary or secondary education or not, your work has value, your output adds to the fabric of your community. Whether you work in a grocery store or work to tear down once great ships, whether you sweep floors or drive a bus, every role we play matters in society. Whether you graduate as a geologist, scientist, a teacher, a sociologist or doctor – every profession at every level has a role to play and can take lessons from one another. The profit a business makes matters as much as what it stands for, how it impacts their stakeholders, the ones they are fortunate to serve, and those that help serve them.

Businesses must more fully appreciate the impact they have on their communities and work to mitigate any detrimental effect they may have. Business leaders should fully understand the importance of their supply chains and their collective production, and drive inclusive practices into how they earn revenue (and thus profit). The companies that optimize stakeholder value – that find purpose with profit – these are the businesses that can go *Beyond Good*.

The profit of purpose

How do we define purpose in the context of business profitability? While any form of profit can drive financial gain for some, it may also mean a loss for others if that profit is not fairly distributed. But business profitability can mean something else entirely. Most cultures normalize forms of appreciation for community and the common good from the earliest years – whether in the context of learning a shared history, understanding what our societies have endured or as part of better understanding cultural norms. This is where many of the principles of *Beyond Good* coalesce.

The idea is that we are all part of something greater, a greater good – one where we can make positive decisions that impact those around us. We are the ones that raise hands in meetings when something seems amiss, we are the ones that ask why one group is favoured over another, challenging any form of bias, unintentional or ingrained; we are the ones that work hard to demonstrate empathy for the needs of others in our community. We are the ones in our organizations who question how revenue is created, how profit is distributed, how wages are determined. It is only through questioning the status quo that we achieve progress. It is only through challenging the existing narrative that we derive purpose.

The questions around profitability are no different. We know that not every business output is going to necessarily be for the common good. Not every enterprise is going to benefit every community. There will be profit allocated less than fairly. It is not a question of whether some businesses that create negative outcomes should exist, but also what those businesses are doing for members of their communities, and how they are taking care of all of their stakeholders. There is no stopping supply and demand, but there is a movement to challenge the status quo of pursuing money over sense, of favouring the common good over negative goods. There must be profit of purpose in the end.

SPOTLIGHT ON B CORPORATIONS: DOING WELL BY DOING GOOD

What is the power of a business to do good? Enter B Corporations,[8] or 'B Corps' as people like to call them. These are corporations that are committed to a new path, a new way forward to change the way they do business towards the arc of the common good. These are businesses that believe there is another way to invest profits into their communities rather than continually extracting value. From Ben & Jerry's Ice Cream to Patagonia, these are enterprises that deform the norm, accelerating a global culture shift to redefine success in business and build a more inclusive and sustainable economy.

Certified B Corporations are businesses that meet the highest standards of verified social and environmental performance, public transparency and legal accountability with the aim of balancing profit and purpose. They believe that society's biggest issues cannot be solved by government and non-profit organizations alone, that there is a place for private businesses to have a positive

---

impact. Their community of businesses focuses on reducing inequality, helping reduce poverty, building a more sustainable and healthier environment, developing stronger and more resilient communities, and creating more high-quality jobs that have purpose. B Corps use profits and growth as a means to a greater end – a positive impact for all their stakeholders: employees, communities and the environment. Some examples include:

- **Ben & Jerry's Ice Cream**
  Ben & Jerry's was one of the first companies in the world to give equal importance to social mission, product and financial goals. From committing to source Fair Trade ingredients to rallying against economic inequality in the US, the ice-cream company, with humble beginnings in Vermont in 1978, has long supported movements that seek to build shared prosperity in society. Central to the mission of Ben & Jerry's is the belief that its social, product and economic missions *must thrive equally in a manner that commands deep respect for individuals in and outside the company and supports the communities of which they are a part.*

- **CNote**
  This FinTech aims to make it easier to invest in a more inclusive economy. They partner with Community Development Financial Institutions (CDFI), and the investments go directly to support community development, funding loans for small businesses owned by women and people of colour, as well as affordable housing, and bringing opportunity to low-income areas. According to CNote, 51 cents out of every dollar invested has funded businesses led by people of colour and 35 cents out of every dollar invested has funded businesses owned by women.

- **Patagonia**
  Since 1985, this outdoor apparel company (and first certified B Corp in the State of California) has pledged 1 per cent of sales to the preservation and restoration of the natural environment around the world. They have awarded over $89 million in cash and in-kind donations to domestic and international

grassroots environmental groups that are making a difference in their local communities, from biodiversity loss to climate action. It was named a UN Champion of the Earth in 2019. Patagonia's goal is to be carbon-neutral by 2025; the company is also moving towards 100 per cent renewable and recycled raw materials. Together with other B Corps, Patagonia has demonstrated that sustainable business is not charity; rather, it can do well while building a better business.

- **Tony's Chocolonely**
  This was founded in 2004 by a Dutch journalist, Teun van de Keuken, as a 'journalist bar', to draw attention to the unethical practices in the chocolate industry.[9] Based in Amsterdam, the Netherlands, Tony's vision is to make 100 per cent slave-free chocolate the norm worldwide. Its packaging and the way cocoa farmers are treated are 100 per cent slave-free, fair and transparent: 'Money is a means, not a goal.' The company leads by example to show that profit and purpose can (and should) co-exist; that it is possible to make slave-free chocolate and be commercially successful through traceable beans, higher prices, strong farmers, focusing on long-term relationships and improved productivity.

The purpose of FinTech – like any industry – is to serve its consumers to the best of its ability. With the available technologies, regulatory support, entrepreneurial spirit and ample talent, the FinTech industry is in a position of strength. But however big or small a FinTech initiative is, however ambitious or niche it is, its aim needs to be clear: to find a practical solution to a problem, to alleviate a pain-point, to bring a tangible improvement, to enable consumers' financial wellbeing. TANYA ANDREASYAN, MD AND EDITOR-IN-CHIEF AT FINTECH FUTURES

SPOTLIGHT ON CREDIT UNIONS AND BUILDING SOCIETIES

We would be remiss if we didn't discuss the importance of the credit union movement in the conversation around profit and inclusive business practices within financial services. As the perfect foil to traditional banks, credit unions are financial cooperatives that function as not-for-profit business entities focused on meeting the financial needs of their members. They are community-focused institutions designed around a simple premise: *people helping people.*

What's the difference between credit unions and banks? It comes down to ownership, control and profit. Each member of a credit union holds a share account of the financial cooperative, representing their share of ownership in the institution. Rather than being controlled by an executive team and shareholders, credit unions have a volunteer board made up of credit-union members who then help guide a management team on how to best serve the needs of their membership. The members of each credit union vote on who represents them on the board. Each member is given one vote, regardless of how much money the member holds in the institution (or how profitable they are).

Members are then simultaneously shareholders and stakeholders in the credit union and, in turn, in the community that the credit union serves. The members' collective savings are available to help the cooperative offer varied forms of deposits, investments, loans and other services to the benefit of the collective membership. Credit unions tend to offer higher rates on savings products and lower rates on loans and offer often superior financial benefits when compared to most banks. Offering simpler product lines and added transparency around associated fees, credit unions play an important role in their communities, especially in serving the needs of those living in low-income areas where many people are underbanked or unbanked.

Why isn't everyone a credit-union member then, if they appear to help people more than banks? Credit-union member growth is tied to how credit unions began and how their field of membership – the breadth of members they are allowed to serve by regulators – has evolved.

Credit unions started in Germany in 1852, when Franz Hermann Schulze-Delitzsch took two initial financial cooperative projects and helped develop the first urban credit-union system.[10] Credit unions and similar community-based financial collectives started to spread into Italy, France, the Netherlands, England, Austria and beyond. In these early years, credit unions were often founded by employers or communities in response to the rising costs of accessing credit. The global credit-union model rapidly evolved, especially when it moved to North America.

The first credit union in North America was founded in Quebec in 1901, and the first in the United States – now representing the largest market for credit unions – was founded in 1908. At the end of 2019, there were 5,236 credit unions serving the financial needs of more than 120 million members in the United States alone, with deposits totalling $1.22 trillion.[11]

Globally, credit unions range in size from small institutions dedicated to the needs of a single family to larger credit unions sponsored by the employees of small and large businesses. There are also many credit unions whose membership is focused geographically on the needs of entire communities. The World Council of Credit Unions (WOCCU) reported that there were 85,400 credit unions in 118 countries at the end of 2018, serving 274.2 million members and entrusted with $2.19 trillion in assets.[12]

With continued growth and a commitment to serving the often underserved, credit unions provide many lessons for today's financial institutions and FinTech startups, among them:

- Credit unions' ownership model and not-for-profit mandate drive an often fanatical focus on the financial needs of their members.
- The value of membership that credit unions provide – the net benefit of the financial relationship – is significant, especially in regard to banks.

- Any perceived shortcomings – whether lacking locational convenience or robust technology – is slowly eroding as more credit unions work together with innovative partners to ensure this cooperative business model evolves.

There are other types of financial cooperatives with similar values, some even older than credit unions themselves. Building societies evolved within the United Kingdom and were originally focused on funding land purchases for their members. The first was started in 1775, with the establishment of Ketley's Building Society, and was terminated once every member was housed. The Building Societies Association represents all 43 UK building societies, as well as 6 credit unions (out of 277), with assets of nearly £430 billion. Together with their subsidiaries, they hold 23 per cent of all funded mortgages (over £335 billion) and 18 per cent of deposits (£295 billion).[13]

Like credit unions, building societies are financial cooperatives that are committed to serving the needs of their community stakeholders, not the needs of shareholders. History provided an interesting lesson in the UK when several not-for-profit building societies switched over to a for-profit banking model, with the promise that their members would benefit in the long term.

Six building societies, in fact, converted to traditional banks after the Conservative government increased competition by allowing existing banks to offer mortgages in the 1980s. These new converts, including Halifax, Northern Rock and Bradford & Bingley, ran into financial trouble during the Great Recession and all six were or either declared bankrupt or sold to other banks (to Banco Santander in the case of the converted Abbey Bank and Alliance & Leicester).

A study of these institutions completed in 2005 found that the members of the converted building societies benefited very little from the business-model conversion. The main benefactors of the entire experiment – no surprise really – were the executives running the institutions when the conversions occurred, whose salaries had increased by 293 per cent between 1993 and 2000.[14]

In cases like these, it seems, seeking profit over purpose can lead to one's demise. The important lesson in these cooperative models is just that: there are alternatives that focus less on profit, and more on ways to meet people's financial needs. This is how the old can become new again, and how we can derive new ways to serve the diverse needs of our communities without worsening an already growing divide between those who have more and those who have less. Inequality is a choice made by the legacy of leaders within any community over time. Every business model can be refocused towards the arc of the common good, even financial services.

SPOTLIGHT ON INCLUSIVE FINTECH BUSINESS MODELS

The financial services industry is an interesting focal point for the question of profit and purpose. The global banking industry has extracted tremendous profit while becoming ingrained in the facilitation of the most basic needs of everyday life. Whether in the form of a traditional bank, a FinTech startup or a component of our financial infrastructure, the way that money and capital investment move within a society is vital to its overall health.

Making money from money is – especially through the friction caused by using money – one of the oldest and surest ways to derive profit. But can financial services also drive a common good and create a positive net impact within our communities? The answer is increasingly 'yes'. FinTech startups, from companies like Ant Group to TransferWise, have led efforts in pushing the industry towards achieving global financial inclusion. Hundreds of startups now focus on providing banking services to those that are underbanked, and thousands more are helping everyday consumers save, invest, optimize spending and make a difference in the finances across generations. Industry incumbents have taken notice, too, and responded with their own efforts to challenge their existing business model – not because it's good public relations, but because it turns out that more inclusive business practices are profitable as well. This is a win-win for the banking industry and consumers.

Omidyar Network, Flourish Ventures and Oliver Wyman studied current revenue practices among financial health entrepreneurs to help them find ways to develop successful revenue models that reinforce, rather than threaten, consumer trust and promote financial health. Their report, 'Breaking New Ground in FinTech: A Primer on Revenue Models that Create Value and Build Trust', highlighted trends from data collected from 350 leading FinTech startups, 11 case studies, advice from founders and investors, focus groups and digital diaries with consumers across income ranges and geographies.[15] The research distills approaches on how to embed commitment to financial health into the company's core strategy and how to mitigate the risks of its revenue model to customers.

The research uncovered specific emerging practices that successfully align revenue with value creation for consumers on a sustainable basis, discusses emerging revenue strategies and provides guiding principles for creating financial-health alignment. The idea is to inspire entrepreneurs serving the mass market and provide them with a framework that opens up the possibility of doing well by doing good. The report details how startups make their profit and the value exchange between their customers and communities. Here are some of the FinTech startups highlighted in the report:

- **Betterment**
  One of the original robo-advisers that reinvented low-cost investment management. Helping add transparency to investing through employee-sponsored 401k retirement plans, startups like Betterment are among the first in this space to aggregate and optimize long-term investments from multiple providers within one dashboard view.

- **Even**

  Helps consumers get paid on demand through select employers, budget instantly based on upcoming bills, and automate savings to meet goals. The company has partnered with large employers such as Walmart to offer Even as a benefit to Walmart employees. Even helps consumers build up emergency savings and lets them tap into these funds when they need them most.

- **Qapital**

  Helps customers with goal-based saving, spending and investing by showing both outcomes (eg amount saved) and work done (eg 148 transfers based on rounding up purchases to the nearest $2) via an activity feed, such as a social network. They were the first financial startup to use the IFTTT application (If This, Then That) to link non-financial behaviour to financial outcome ('If I walk five miles, add $5 to my savings account').

- **Stash**

  Digital financial services platform for those new to investing. It built a tool around simplicity, ease of use and education that was a key source of value created for users. Stash uses behavioural science to message users with both financial tips and advice in order to nudge them to save and invest more for the long term by shifting their short-term behaviours.

- **Truebill**

  Helps consumers track their bills, cancel unwanted subscriptions and request refunds. Apps like Truebill (and the equally impressive BillShark) help customers manage down the impact of the subscription economy (streaming services like Netflix, utility bills, internet and mobile-phone bills) to improve the financial health of their customers.

As the (now) old phrase goes 'there's now an app for that', and banking is no different. With the influx of FinTech startups like these over the decade since the Great Recession, the financial services industry has changed to move towards these models of targeted financial inclusion. While there is still a long way to go towards building an industry-wide model dedicated to every level of society, the coronovirus pandemic will only hasten this move towards broader services and more transparent business models.

The problem with large banks and their historical (often negative) impact on the economic equality of our communities, has much to do with their focus on short-term profitability and a lack of empathy from their executive teams. Rather than expecting banking to change itself, we must support external change that will force the hand of the industry and make it more responsive to the needs of its communities and to the arc of the common good.

While admitting that identifying a responsible revenue model was no simple task, the report's goal was to inspire entrepreneurs to invest early in developing sustainable revenue models. In doing so, they will continue to build robust businesses that develop solutions to improve consumer financial health, have a permanent and positive impact on the financial-services industry, and derive sustainable profit that only strengthens the communities they serve.

The purpose of FinTech is a tantalizing proposition: it aims to redefine an industry in need of it. Fintech, at its best, is trying to democratize finance. The banking industry is in the middle of an existential crisis and must dream up new value propositions. FinTech, while not always a hero, is putting extra pressure on the industry to create something better across all kinds of products and services. MARY WISNIEWSKI, BANKING EDITOR AND FINTECH FEATURES REPORTER AT BANKRATE

SPOTLIGHT ON TECHNOLOGY PLATFORMS AND PROFIT

We are in the midst of a fundamental shift in the global business environment. Large technology platforms – Apple, Google, Facebook, Amazon, Baidu, Tencent, Alibaba, Ant Group, JD.com,

Didi and others – now control much of our everyday lives. They encompass everything from the bundling of everyday activities embedded into superapps (from ordering food to booking a trip) to payments, social networks and the devices themselves. With that in mind, we must examine what these business models and their immense levels of profitability mean to our society. While regulators are focused on necessary checks of power around consumer privacy and securing trade secrets, as users of these systems we should also be concerned about how our personal data, preferences and daily activities are now empowering the profit flywheels of these companies.

In his thought-provoking book, *Winners Take All: The elite charade of changing the world*, Anand Giridharadas questions the current power structure of today's global stage, including that of the large technological firms such as those mentioned above, as well as the global elite that empowers them. More interestingly, he questions the opportunity cost of a society controlled by the actions of fewer and fewer companies and more and more billionaires. What do these companies do with our data, what does this mean for competition of ideas and for the opportunity cost of competition lost to these large networks? What does this mean for the future of society?

We live in a time of transformative economic conditions, which combine the power of technological solutions led by algorithms with increasingly empathy-led decision-making capabilities. Will technology lead to better outcomes in the long run? Could the current monopolistic scale of these technology platforms improve the common good? What are we missing that could have been built instead?

We should all care about what our most talented engineers and coders are up to and what large technology firms are focused on because it will eventually impact all of us. We should scrutinize the business models of these companies and the investments of venture capitalists just as we would the actions of owners of the local corner store, because what these firms do impacts our lives and our communities, our work and consumption trends, and the distribution of profit back into our society. In every way possible, we should challenge growing profit margins, consolidation of businesses, executive pay and the existing system that lauds success of valuation over the success of our communities.

We should support the efforts of entrepreneurs that are fundamentally addressing underlying systemic problems such as wage inequality, expanded job training, education inequality, broadband access and other means to smooth out the impact of luck on who has the opportunity to succeed. We must help these efforts move beyond thoughts to actions; we must move from customer research that focuses on exploiting people for profit to an understanding of the root causes of the problems that are systemic to the business model, to our communities and the stakeholders that we are fortunate to serve. Revolutions are ongoing evolutions of thoughts and broad strokes of actions that start on a tiny three-inch screen of glass and the glowing screens in cafés and newsrooms.

The impact of technological change is here to stay, and we should expect no less than more equitable distribution of profit from the large technology platforms for our society. This means that as users of these systems and consumers of their output, we have a way to collectively influence what is built – through our actions and activities within these networks. If we can't rally people to acknowledge their privilege and unite together to improve the lives of others, then what kind of society have we become? The principles of *Beyond Good* encourage us to think beyond ourselves and beyond limitations by addressing the underlying issues that impact our communities, and technology is no exception. We have the power to drive change, both through individual actions and through our influence as leaders.

Remittances can represent up to 40 per cent of GDP in third world countries. FinTech enables money movement and financial support to supplement wages for the underpaid and the underbanked so they can pay for their basic needs. STEPHANIE FOSTER, WOMEN DRIVING INNOVATION

The empathy model

What if we moved the economics of capitalism and other economic models from taking care of shareholders first to taking care of stakeholders always? What would that look like in practice, specifically in financial services, in technology and other industries we've discussed? Across the globe today, more companies are recognizing that doing well by doing good simply means acknowledging that their primary function is doing everything they can to meet the increasingly complex needs of the communities they serve. Empathy can be at the centre of a business model because it has heart and humanity as its guide.

We must be intentional in pursuing innovations that address the social challenges that we face as a civilization. The onus is on all of us to ensure that we are building an equitable future that will deliver positive outcomes for everyone. At the heart of *Beyond Good* is this optimism. It comes from our conversations with people across the world doing amazing things within their companies and communities to help others. They offer us hope.

But we know change and progress do not come easily. Change requires work, perseverance and commitment. Progress also requires us to confront the truth of inequality. This may start with questions around profitability and purpose, but it quickly becomes more personal.

We must understand our value to society, the roles that we personally play and the ways in which our business models impact our communities. To be critical is not to be cynical. It is to probe and not pretend things cannot be better. It is to do more than hope – it is to provide a path towards action. It is not to just talk about the common good, but to draw a map towards it.

The pursuit of purpose for the greater good is the purest form of action we can aspire to, to take the steps necessary to inspire change and be a voice for greater equality. This is what we have tried to do by sharing these stories and ideas. Our only hope is that you can find ways to incorporate them into your own actions, to find the hope that you need to keep going, and make the world just that much better for someone else.

CHAPTER SEVEN

Leadership for good

The way to right wrongs is to turn the light of truth upon them.[1] IDA B WELLS

A different path indeed

What does leadership mean to you? In *Good to Great*, Jim Collins characterizes successful leaders as those who concentrate on activities that they are deeply passionate about and who cement their legacy by ensuring that their companies remain committed to what they can be the best in the world at, focused on creating their internal flywheel to drive their economic engine, with revenue and profitability the primary drivers. But is this the right end game? Is this the right lesson for leaders today? How do we develop more leaders that create businesses and shift business models that previously stemmed from the concepts of 'good to great' towards ones focused on the greater good? How do we take the principles of B Corporations and apply them to principles of leadership?

As we discussed in the last chapter, revenue and profit cannot be the best measurement of effective management, and surely they cannot be the only set of metrics, regardless of which macroeconomic model a society falls under. The focus on rapid growth ('hockey stick' growth as they call it in Silicon Valley, as users rocket upwards), the creation of scale and moats, the short-term horizons and the maximizing of shareholder value represent trade-offs, ones that negatively impact far too many elements of our communities.

Collins argues that these growth-focused activities create positive cultural forces that help propel organizations forward, towards perpetual success – similar to the concept of trickle-down economics, where advantages provided to the wealthy will trickle down benefits to the masses. But this isn't the time for Adam Smith and his invisible hand. This doesn't feel right for this moment, nor for the world we live in now. There are too many needs that remain unfulfilled; our state of economy demands a different approach.

How we prepare the next generation of leaders matters. As does how we shift attention towards more principled and tangible demonstrations of collective management that embraces the needs of the entirety of our communities. With the changes taking place in society and the relentless pace of technology, shifting mindsets is an increasingly difficult task. Yet we must try. This is the time for long-needed structural change within the businesses in our communities. This moment will be our turning point in the evolution of leadership for good.

Finding new meaning in a new world

At the risk of antagonizing our readers, we ask again: What does leadership mean to you? And if we were to ask you to name the essential qualities of a *good leader*, what would those qualities be? Who do you aspire to emulate? What individuals or organizations come to mind? And more importantly, why? What characteristics or actions left the deepest impression? We ask for a reason. Because the world that we've written about has changed – yet again.

As we were writing this book, the Covid-19 pandemic was thrust upon humanity. While the crisis was far from over at the time of writing, there have already been many lessons learned from how we work, where we work and how society treats its most vulnerable citizens and its most essential workers. This moment of uncertainty offers a tangible moment of clarity.

It is much easier to lead in times of prosperity than in times of chaos. As we look around us, we are confronted with challenges, such as this pandemic, that at least initially felt insurmountable. From unrest stemming from geopolitical conflicts and growing inequalities to natural disasters, climate crisis and coronavirus, humanity is being tested like never before. Will we emerge stronger and rebuild better? Or will the pieces be put back together in disarray? Leadership in times of crisis tests the best of us. But it also presents us with the greatest opportunity to make a positive impact – enabling meaningful contributions to change the world for good.

True leaders come from all walks of life, unbound by titles or job descriptions. With much of the world's citizens socially and physically isolated from each other, emotionally and physically exhausted from the dual demands of daily life and an uncertain future, a simple 'you are not alone' carries more weight than ever. But effective leadership goes beyond words and empathy. It requires acknowledging what is not working; and taking bold actions to challenge us to take an unproven path.

As we think more about the next iteration of leadership in our communities, we discuss what we've learned from this global pandemic, then shift focus back to small-business creation, incubation, the funding of ideas (especially those outside of Silicon

Valley) and the implications for leadership as the impact of gig work on a global scale evolves. In this chapter and the next, we review some of these challenges that lie ahead of us and relate stories of leaders and organizations who help propel us on our journey to go *Beyond Good*.

A crisis of definition

It was the best of times, then suddenly, it was the worst. There is nothing quite like a global pandemic to recast the lives of billions – as we prayed for medical solutions to temper the impact of this microscopic scourge on our species; as we watched in sadness the growing numbers of cases and deaths related to this virus; as we marvelled at the tireless efforts of our medical professionals and those among us selflessly aiding their communities; as we redefined the meaning of truly essential workers and navigated the future realities of the workplace and that of our educational infrastructure; as we longed for the lost connectivity to our friends and our family and those that we love. As we've looked forward to a return to normal, fully knowing it will have to be a very different normal, we've collectively clung to one word that will define a future not yet written – *hope*. And let's be clear, no one knows still what is next.

Our leaders have had to refocus, just as our communities had to prepare for whatever is next. Beyond the physical and economic devastation caused by the Covid-19 virus and its growing toll on humanity, this very unexpected period of social isolation has triggered much soul-searching for our leaders. It's as if a genie has been uncorked and enveloped much of the world with equal doses of compassion, melancholy and perturbation. This pandemic has provided an opportunity for all of us to more fully appreciate and acknowledge our connections to one another. It has prompted much-needed private and public dialogue about what we do and about how much our actions, innate propensities and work matter, and how much does not. The pandemic will continue to be an opportunity to redefine our societies and our communities, and redefine the role of leadership itself; to turn that longing for hope for so many into one of action that impacts us all. There are numerous lessons that leaders must take from this crisis.

Remote work and digital divide

The world, as we know it, came to a standstill as the pandemic spread. Businesses closed their offices. Schools cancelled classes. Well-off city dwellers decamped to their holiday homes far away from crowds. While remote workers struggled with marathon virtual-collaboration sessions, working parents navigated the sea of apps to support their children's virtual learning.

But not everyone could do their work remotely, not every child could continue their learning virtually. The pandemic widened the disparity between the haves and the have nots; it shed light on the racial, income and geographical divide. As we have learned, the ability to work and learn remotely is a privilege not a right. It is a privilege afforded to only a portion of our communities.

In the US, the majority of those who lacked internet access were Black and Hispanic, those who lived in rural areas, or those who came from low-income households. Based on figures from a study by the Joint Center For Political and Economic Studies, 34 per cent of Black adults in the US do not have home broadband.[2] In addition, 30.6 per cent of Black households with one or more children aged 17 or younger (over 3.25 million Black children) lack high-speed home internet. In rural areas around the globe, children had to leverage internet access from wherever they could, even along the side of roads – just to receive their education.

According to a study from Essence, '85 per cent of Black women who are parents say there are not enough computers or laptops in their household to support the educational needs of their children, and 79 per cent say their children are not getting enough support from their school systems.'[3] Imagine the longer-term impact on these families when much of the nation's education was forced to become virtual.

Their worries are well-founded. In a national survey of US teachers and school district leaders administered by *Education Week*, 'more than half (64 per cent) of surveyed district leaders from high-poverty districts (more than 75 per cent of the low-income student population) said technology access is a major challenge to learning during extended school shutdowns.'[4]

Teachers in the highest-poverty schools also report that 'nearly a third of their students are not logging in or otherwise making contact.' And rural schools in particular face the further challenge of poor connectivity, limited staff and technical expertise – factors that have shaped our public education and hence its inequities prior to Covid-19.

The challenge extends beyond the homework gap suffered by the millions of children attending primary and secondary schools. As universities begin switching from in-person classes to virtual classrooms, those from lower socio-economic communities increasingly find themselves struggling to succeed in a remote-learning environment owing to lack of broadband access, exacerbating the inequalities in our society that higher education aims to solve. Broadband access is not a luxury; it is a necessity.

President Obama remarked the following, during a visit to Cedar Falls, Iowa, in 2015: 'This isn't just about making it easier to stream Netflix... This is about helping local businesses grow and prosper and compete in a global economy. It's about giving the entrepreneur, the small businessperson on Main Street a chance to compete with the folks out in Silicon Valley, or across the globe. It's about helping a student access the online courses and employment opportunities that can help her pursue her dreams.'[5]

Unfortunately, such challenges are not unique to the United States. Similar barriers exist in other developed economies where classes of people are marginalized because of their age, ethnicity, gender identity and other factors. In Canada, for example, high cost and demographic differences, especially within the Northern Territories, have also resulted in disparity in online connectivity.

According to figures from the Communications Monitoring Report, 1 in 10 Canadian households still have no internet at home.[6] And perhaps unsurprisingly, those who are hit the hardest are the ones living in rural and remote communities, the First Nation reserve areas, the official minority language communities (OLMCs), as well as the low-income families.

Similar stories unfold in India, where fixed broadband is at 1.5 active subscriptions per 100 inhabitants only, compared to the global average of 14.9.[7] And there remains a stark divide between urban and rural areas.[8] Lack of reliable and available broadband connectivity threatens to increase the economic divide across class, gender and region. Which begs the question, can these communities fully participate in the digital economy when they lack even the most basic access? What have we learned from the pandemic that leaders can leverage to ensure more communities are digitally enabled?

Caregiving and gender equity

The Covid-19 pandemic has exposed – even intensified – gender inequality in our society. While we are still in the midst of this crisis and the long-term impact is unknown, the preliminary data is not promising. With disrupted school routines, parents are being asked to navigate the unchartered waters of remote work and full-time childcare. Consider the following data points from Mercer, a US human resources consulting firm, and part of the family of Marsh & McLennan Companies:[9]

- Full-time working mothers in two-parent households are on average doing around 22 hours of childcare a week during Covid-19, in addition to maintaining their jobs.

- One in five working parents said that either they or their partner are considering leaving the workforce to care for their children.

According to the IMF, women are hit the hardest by the uncertainty stemming from the pandemic and the resulting deep recession. The May job report in Canada 'shows that women's employment increased by 1.1 per cent compared with 2.4 per cent for men, as childcare issues persist. Furthermore, among parents with at least one child under the age of six, men were roughly three times more likely to have returned to work than women.'[10]

Data from Microsoft published in the *Harvard Business Review* also suggests that our working days are getting longer and more fragmented:

- Weekly meeting time has increased by 10% overall.
- A new 'night shift' has taken root: instant messaging increased by 52% between 6pm and midnight.
- Work–life boundaries have blurred, with more employees working over the weekends.[11]

Not only is this unsustainable, but it will also result in further burnout, set back the hard-earned progress in women's economic opportunities, and even widen the gender disparity for women, since they typically bear the brunt of the domestic housework. And that is only for parents who have the privilege of remote work, which is not an option available to everyone. Some organizations, such as the Florida State University, specifically prohibits childcare during remote work. Such policies are often made with erroneous assumptions that there is a support system (ie caregivers and spouses) that is flexible, adaptable and available at all times – an assumption that is not only outdated, but one that impacts women and families of colour the most.

According to Pew Research, the United States has the world's highest rate of children living in single-parent households, with nearly a quarter of US children under the age of 18 living with one parent and no other adults. Of all the single-parent families in the US, single mothers make up the majority, with nearly 30 per cent of their families living under the poverty line, compared with 62 per cent of families with married parents. Families where the father is the sole breadwinner make up only about a quarter of families (27 per cent) with children under 18.[12]

To make matters worse, many women hold jobs in areas such as healthcare that are deemed essential during the pandemic. Without affordable childcare options, our society is increasingly asking these working mothers to choose between taking care of their children and putting food on the table. Is that really an option?

SPOTLIGHT ON MICROSOFT'S SKILLS INITIATIVE

A key to recovery from the pandemic is to help those who have been disproportionately impacted by Covid-19 and the economic downturn; this includes women, those from low-income households and under-represented minorities.

In June 2020, Microsoft announced a skills initiative to help 25 million people worldwide acquire digital skills, including free access to content across the vast Microsoft ecosystem – GitHub, LinkedIn and Microsoft, for example – in order to develop the skills needed for in-demand jobs and connect job seekers to opportunities through industry-recognized certifications and tools. The programme will also include $20 million in cash grants for non-profit organizations worldwide, including community-based non-profits led by and serving communities of colour in the United States.[13]

Such an undertaking is not without precedence; take, for example, the SkillsFuture initiative that we highlighted in the first chapter. Other examples include the Work-Sharing Program in Canada, where employees agree to a reduced work schedule and share the available work for a specified time; salary is compensated for those in the programme who participate in skills training during the time periods missed.

> Meeting the challenges of today and demands of the future will require us to approach education and learning differently. Employers have as much a role to play as employees; more private and public partnerships are needed to ensure that training is available to everyone in society, especially those whose jobs are more vulnerable to automation and do not have access to opportunities or new career options. The time is now for us to close the opportunity gap and create new pathways of opportunities for everyone. Every technology firm large and small can learn something from Microsoft's leadership.

Now more than ever, AI has the potential of harnessing the social fabric of society; helping us to identify the inequities, the challenges we need to solve, and more accurately predict things that might happen. Technology is really at the heart of getting us to be a socially and culturally aware society. Through skilling and reskilling, we are able to create access to opportunity and ensure that no one is left behind. JACKY WRIGHT, CHIEF DIGITAL OFFICER AND CORPORATE VP, MICROSOFT US

Making the future of work equitable

While the pandemic is unprecedented and organizations are simply scrambling to cope, there are many lessons that we can take on board to make the future of remote work more equitable. To reduce interruptions, some companies have instituted quiet days, where they encourage employees to take time off or block the time off from meetings so that they can focus without work interruptions. Flexible work arrangements to allow employees to work around personal responsibilities such as childcare were always important before the pandemic, and have become even more so now that many schools are closed. Subsidized childcare, whether on-site or in-home, can also help to reduce the burden on working parents, especially those who bear the sole responsibility of child-caring. Companies must recognize the importance of employee wellbeing and acknowledge the quality of work being done is far more important than the actual hours that work is being done.

The move by some technology companies to allow extended remote work is certainly a welcoming gesture for many employees who are either concerned about their health or are struggling to find caregiving options. With or without the pandemic, flexible work arrangements should be the future model of work. Having a decentralized workforce, and allowing employees to work from home, enables companies to tap into local talented people, who cannot afford to or are unable to relocate.

From a policy perspective, we must recognize the importance of caregiving and the needs of working parents, especially those who are the most vulnerable: the single parents and the low-income families. As we rebuild for a more resilient future, we must take into account the need for affordable and available caregiving options, as well as paid family leave. We need inclusive economic policies that preserve employment linkages and extend safety nets for the vulnerable members of our society. These are not women's issues; rather, they are vital to the success of our economic recovery.

We must also do more to bridge the digital divide and invest in education, to allow more people to benefit from the digital economy and create a more inclusive and equitable recovery for all. Digital inclusion is economic inclusion. Having access to digital tools and technology is no longer a nice-to-have; it is essential for economic and social mobility. Else, we risk leaving behind the very same communities that technology has the potential to equalize and enable.

SPOTLIGHT ON DIGITAL CHARLOTTE

Launched in 2011, Digital Charlotte was 'developed as a component in the Queen's Knight School's Master Plan to strengthen digital and media literacy in Charlotte', recognizing that delivering literacy resources to communities in Charlotte is a crucial step in empowering the success of the city.

The initiative is part of the Charlotte Digital Inclusion Alliance (CDIA), supported by a grant from the John S and James L Knight Foundation. The alliance is focused on developing a more digitally inclusive and equitable future, making technology accessible to everyone in the Charlotte community, with a goal of reducing the digital divide across Mecklenburg County from 19 per cent to 9 per cent by 2026.

A 2013 study from Harvard University and UC Berkeley ranked Charlotte-Mecklenburg *50th out of 50* in upward mobility for children born into the lowest income quintile in the area.[14] Broadband access is a crucial success factor to social and economic mobility; however, according to the organization's own estimates, and highlighted in Charlotte Digital Inclusion Alliance's Digital Inclusion Playbook, 'nearly 20 per cent of residents in Charlotte do not have internet at home, nor the means to purchase it in the future.'[15] The adoption is uneven, especially among the lower-income families and the African American and Hispanic population in the Charlotte area.

The playbook is a living and breathing document that outlines the areas of focus, goals and initiatives, including public wifi deployment, support programmes for grandparents and caregivers to remove barriers to technology, workforce development and various training programmes.

The crucial work that the alliance provides can serve as a blueprint for other municipalities to follow. According to the FCC Broadband Deployment Report, 21.3 million people do not have access to broadband.[16] But according to Microsoft, after accounting for those with slow or unreliable internet connections, as many as 162.8 million people are not using the internet at broadband speeds, which is more than half the population of the entire US.[17] The time is now to provide affordable broadband access, devices and digital literacy training to these families, from rural communities to urban poor, so that they, too, can be part of the connected ecosystem.

Growing wealth disparity

The wealth disparity in our societies has grown even more stark during the Covid-19 pandemic. After the second quarter of 2020, the stock market not only recovered, but exceeded the highest levels set before the pandemic. But we have to remember – and this is true for every economy – the stock market isn't the real economy. It represents only a portion of the impact on our communities, neighbourhoods and businesses. While the US sustained the highest unemployment in history, the total wealth of the US's billionaires grew $845 billion, or 29 per cent, since the start of the pandemic, according to data from inequality.org. While these numbers are staggering, they are unfortunately not surprising, since much of the wealth of these billionaires is stock-related.[18]

In fact, according to a separate report from the Economic Policy Institute (EPI), in 2019, the ratio of CEO-to-typical-worker compensation was 320-to-1, up from 61-to-1 in 1989 and 21-to-1 in 1965. From 1978 to 2019, CEO pay based on realized compensation grew by a staggering 1,167 per cent, compared to 13.7 per cent for a typical worker. What is particularly stunning is that such outsized growth of the senior executives' compensation is even more pronounced than the growth of the stock market according to the EPI report. It is no wonder that the top 1 per cent of earners have been more than able to recover from the last financial crisis as the stock market and profits soar to new heights.[19] The growth of income and associated wealth has become increasingly unbalanced.

Sources of resilience

Gig economy workers' financial wellbeing is also increasingly under pressure owing to the impact from Covid-19 and the economic crisis, the need for social distancing and lockdowns, as well as the change in consumer habits. As mentioned in earlier chapters, contingent workers such as e-hailing drivers and delivery workers often don't earn enough and are more susceptible to economic shocks owing to the lack of a financial cushion. And the impact is worldwide.

Based on a series of studies being conducted by Flourish Ventures: 'The Digital Hustle: Gig Worker Financial Lives Under Pressure', we learned that gig workers around the world are living on the edge:

- Over two-thirds of Brazilian gig workers now earn less than $200 per month, compared to fewer than 10% before the pandemic – an eightfold increase.

  - Nearly 90% of gig workers lost income since the lockdown began in March 2020, and 78% reported a decline in quality of life, driven by decreased income and inability to pay expenses.

  - In the face of hardship, many gig workers are cutting consumption and using savings. Yet, half of the gig workers indicated that 'they could not cover expenses for a week without borrowing money if they lost their main source of income.'[20]

- Nearly 87% of gig workers in India now earn less than $200 per month, compared to 10% before the pandemic.

  - Women continue to be underserved by the gig economy owing to unequal access to digital technology and under-representation in the workforce.

- Over half of workers could cover household expenses for more than a month without borrowing money if they lost their main source of income.[21]

- The findings in Indonesia are equally devastating. Gig workers from home-health providers to ride-sharing have seen a sharp decline in income since the pandemic, with 79% now earning less than $100 per month. Interestingly, unlike with other economies, there are no notable gender disparities.

  - Perhaps not surprisingly, with 58% of respondents reporting that they could not cover household expenses for a month without borrowing money, these gig workers are more concerned about the impact on their livelihoods than their health.[22]

- A similar story is unfolding for gig workers in South Africa, with approximately four out of five workers now earning less than $240 per month, compared to 16% before the pandemic.

  - 76% of respondents experienced a large decrease in income, with ride-hailing drivers being hit the hardest.

  - Nearly 60% of gig workers reported that they could not cover household expenses for a month without borrowing money if they lost their main source of income.

To cope in the short term, these gig workers need access to money to cover day-to-day needs, from paying off debt to supporting themselves and their families. For the long term, however, they need to attain a more secure financial future by gaining new (digital) skills, starting/growing a business and getting access to tools to plan for emergencies and save for longevity.

One thing that this global pandemic has made very clear is that our lives and livelihoods need more sources of resilience, better cooperation within our communities and more coordination of empathy-led assistance in order for a larger number of people to thrive under even more adverse conditions. This starts with extra support for small businesses and more ways to support entrepreneurship in more places.

Community viability redefined

Small businesses are the backbone of economies worldwide. In China, small and micro businesses collectively account for 94 per cent of all business entities, employing 70 per cent of the Chinese population and contributing close to 60 per cent of China's GDP in 2016. In 2018, there were more than 60 million individually owned businesses. Yet, many of these businesses were not generally well served by banks owing to their relatively small size.

Similarly, in the US, small businesses comprise 99.9 per cent of all businesses, employ nearly 60 million Americans and drive 44 per cent of the economic activity, according to the Small Business Administration Office of Advocacy.[23] The vast majority (78.5 per cent) represent businesses without employees (sole proprietorships). Owing to economic conditions induced by Covid-19, small businesses face a slew of challenges, with 76 per cent having had cash-flow shortages, according to the Independent Community Bankers of America (ICBA; the primary trade group for small US banks).

To make matters worse, Black businesses are more severely impacted compared to those owned by whites, according to the New York Federal Reserve. Aside from suffering from pre-existing economic gaps and weaker cash positions, lack of access to stimulus funding also plays a crucial role. Instead of funnelling the money to places where it is needed the most, loans from the PPP (Paycheck Protection Program), the US Government's signature relief programme for small businesses, flow mostly to companies with the best banking relationships, resulting in significant coverage gaps especially for Black- and Latinx-owned businesses, which traditionally have weaker banking ties. As a result, according to data from the Federal Reserve of New York, in 2020 these loans reached only 20 per cent of eligible firms in states with the highest densities of Black-owned firms, and in counties with the densest Black-owned business activity, coverage rates were typically lower than 20 per cent.[24]

Even before the pandemic, according to a report from the Center for Global Policy Solutions in 2016, it was estimated that 'the US is forgoing an estimated 1.1 million businesses owned by people of colour because of past and present discrimination in American society. These missing businesses could have produced an estimated 9 million more jobs and boosted the national income by $300 billion.'[25]

An inclusive society that enables entrepreneurs to thrive, regardless of the colour of their skin and their socio-economic status, is not only fair, but an enabler for expanded economic growth, allowing minority-owned businesses to contribute more to the growth and recovery of our society. By looking through the lens of entrepreneurship in a different light, we see how much bias is built into the businesses and applications created within our communities, and why it matters that leaders create opportunities for people of colour and communities often less represented.

Other valleys of opportunity

Where we fund, build and incubate ideas matters. In order to develop more inclusive businesses, ones that can flourish and address the needs of more local communities, we need to seed more cities and regions with what made Silicon Valley the heart of innovation for so many decades:

- venture capital and investment;
- infrastructure and technology;

- extensive university and research network;
- government incentives;
- access to a diverse and trained workforce.

Rather than attempting to replicate Silicon Valley, many areas have embraced the ethos and ingredients of the San Francisco Bay Area and made it their own. Take, for example, the so-called 'Silicon Slopes' in Utah's Salt Lake City area (one of its startups, MX, is profiled in Chapter 8), and hundreds of other cities and regions globally now vying for talent, capital and the consolidation of great ideas of thousands of startups. Areas of startup development include Tokyo, Singapore, Hong Kong, Shenzhen, Beijing, Bengaluru, Tel Aviv, Stockholm, Moscow, Amsterdam, Berlin, Paris, Lisbon, London, Boston and New York. Many of these cities combine the ingredients of Silicon Valley and act as a gravitational pull for additional startup activity.

In the case of Hong Kong, the development of the Greater Bay Area is an interesting showcase of private/public partnership. The region comprises Hong Kong, Macao and nine municipalities from Mainland China. Development of new zones, currently underway, includes an Innovation and Technology Hub for frontier technologies such as artificial intelligence; this hub can leverage the talent from Hong Kong and its status as a key financial hub.

Another good example is the Founders Factory, with offices in London, Johannesburg, Paris and New York. They partner with founders working to scale up startups across regions. What is interesting about their model is that they combine both a venture studio and an accelerator. The venture studio helps founders build their startup idea from scratch or they can apply to build off one of the Founders Factory existing projects. After successfully applying to the venture studio, teams are given a £100,000 initial fund and around a six-month runway to work on the idea with the embedded team. Their accelerator helps startups with an existing product in the market gain additional traction and seek additional funding. Founders Fund also works with 11 corporates, including Avica, easyJet, L'Oréal and M&S, to build on ideas in their respective markets. They have helped startups like BRB (Be Right Back, a travel app), Bower Collective (an e-commerce platform for home and personal-care products) and Entale (an audio-storytelling development).

In terms of more diverse ideas and more community-focused startups, looking outside of larger cities also seems to be gaining momentum with venture capitalists as well. Arunkumar (Arun) Krishnakumar, partner at Green Shores Capital, based in London, and author of *Quantum Computing and Blockchain in Business*,[26] sees the opportunity this way: 'As a VC, you are constantly on the lookout for an outlier. From an investor's perspective that can feel like looking for a needle in a haystack. I find deals coming out of the smaller cities and towns a lot more interesting. They are often less perfect, but refreshing, with authentic solutions born out of local problems. Purely from an investment perspective, the small city startup can have a more attractive valuation. By leaving out these startups, investors are invariably leaving money on the table.'

As Arun points out, the locations beyond big cities are often more interesting. To combat the rising costs of living in places like Tokyo or New York or Hong Kong, cities well outside major metropolitan areas are seeing an increased focus on innovative startups. We profile one of those here – Venture Center, based in Little Rock, Arkansas, in the southern part of the United States.

SPOTLIGHT ON VENTURE CENTER

The Venture Center is a nonprofit organization in Little Rock, whose mission is to inspire social and economic change in Arkansas. It was launched in May 2014 by a group of entrepreneurs and local business leaders to develop and grow technology startups and talent for central Arkansas and beyond.

It currently operates two FinTech accelerator programmes, in partnership with the ICBA and Fidelity National Information Services, Inc (FIS; a financial technology provider). Through its vast network of mentors and access to financial services executives, the programme has successfully helped its accelerator alumni raise over $250 million in private equity, and generate over $100 million in revenue since 2014, according to Venture Center's own data. Most importantly, the programme has successfully demonstrated that innovation can come from all corners of our society and from all walks of life, and that one size does not fit all.

From drawing inspiration from ancient social banking traditions to creating human-centred AI for banks, the diverse cohorts from the Venture Center programmes have gained exposure and go-to-market opportunities, while bringing new technologies to financial institutions and making tangible impacts in the unique areas of communities that they serve. Perhaps there might be a way to do things differently from Silicon Valley after all.

Our connections to each other and to everything else

The global pandemic may be a wake-up call to a new age, one where the value of our work and the leadership we can provide is reflected in improvements to the community to which we belong. One way in which we can succeed in building a very different future – one much more equitable – is to appreciate how interdependent we really are, how everything in our life is a series of connected systems, both big and small. And that it is within our grasp to bend their functions towards a better way.

While we all make personal connections during our lifetimes, the truth is that we are all connected in ways often both unseen and unforeseen. Everything we see, everything we feel, everything that will be comes from something created before us. Our communities are like this, too, connected by the individuals, families, small businesses and business models that have built up our society, our economic systems, our values and our beliefs – all across the connected expanse of time. Life has always been about much more than any one of us. It's time for us to lead accordingly.

Waste not, want not

'Never let a good crisis go to waste,' is a line often attributed to Churchill, within the context of the ending of the Second World War, and the optimism he felt in defeating fascism alongside Roosevelt and Stalin. As a lesson for leaders, this simple yet powerful phrase sounds like an oxymoron. What good could possibly come out of a crisis? Isn't that why they call it a crisis? The thing about these moments is that it creates a sense of urgency – there is an action for every reaction.

A crisis like the current pandemic, or an economic one like the Great Recession, makes us snap to attention, deal with the pressing issues and look for ways to capitalize on the moment by improving the road ahead. There is no other choice. Leaders across industries think about how to make their companies stronger. Investors reassess their long-term positions as down arrows eventually point up. Technology firms and startups find new forms of efficiencies, new business models and new flywheels.

We should look at the pandemic this way as well and not waste the opportunities that it has thrown at us. The moment should be met with an equal sense of urgency and optimism. Where are the opportunities, as more resources become available, as regulations become more flexible? At moments such as the pandemic, business leaders pay more attention, they are more accessible and more creative in response. This is why we see so many companies being formed after a period of trauma. Times like this make us think differently. There is a sense that the once impossible is now very possible.

The pandemic, the biggest global shock since the Second World War, has been a moment of the utmost gravity, a moment where leaders across all industries must rethink what really matters. It is the opportune time to challenge both societal assumptions and the cadence of our lives and our work, the actions and behaviours of industries, brands and leadership.

As we look outside – from a safe, socially distanced place – can we imagine a better world beyond today? Can we imagine a better future? Can we envision leaders doing so much more? It feels that this is the opportunity for redemption and that there are so many ways to create value for society rather than to continue extracting it. Can our leaders help make things better for more people this time around? If we can only think differently enough our communities will be built back better indeed. This crisis is one with much too high a cost to waste.

CHAPTER EIGHT

A way forward

A shared vision is not an idea... it is rather, a force in people's hearts... at its simplest level, a shared vision is the answer to the question 'What do we want to create?'[1] PETER SENGE

The impossible made possible

As our business climate changes and we face new challenges and opportunities, how can leaders develop a broader mindset and solutions that help lift up more people in our communities? How do we create an environment that allows the art of the impossible made possible to become the norm? How do we go from moments of uncertainty to movements of optimism and hope? It starts with listening, in becoming more aware of what surrounds us, and in finding true purpose.

Change doesn't really happen on its own, but sometimes all it takes is a spark. When you discover your purpose and pursue it with passion, you are more likely to become part of that change you seek to make in the world. We have had the privilege to speak to many startup founders and corporate leaders in the past year, both on our more than one hundred episodes of our 'One Vision' podcast and in the writing of this book during the initial stages of the coronavirus pandemic. In all these inspiring conversations a few things stood out about the character of the people behind the companies, and in the missions they pursue.

The first was compassion and curiosity. Most of these leaders demonstrated that they were continually learning and growing to further understand and fulfil the needs of others. They were genuinely concerned about the inequality they saw firsthand, the lack of attention to corners of their communities left behind. The second was great reflection and personal connectivity to a problem that prompted them to action. In these thoughtful discussions, we heard about solutions such as those designed to improve financial inclusion through payments and credit, ways that made government benefit programmes more efficient and emerging technologies that offer older adults more automated protections from financial scams.

In each interview, there was an acknowledgement of obstacles that impact us all, regardless of whether it was direct or indirect. There was an awareness that we are a community of interconnected parts, all of which matter. In each solution discussed and each personal story we heard there was a focus on thinking more broadly, and taking action to improve the lives of others in very specific ways. In using their examples throughout *Beyond Good*, we have tried to capture the spark that prompted their purpose.

These examples also demonstrate the need to become more proactive. We must acknowledge that our organizations and our communities need to act as one organism of connected systems. Some elements we have to react to – the global pandemic we've been experiencing is an obvious example – but surely there are others that also demand action. Our aging populations, for example, act as a slow-moving storm that should cause more of a reaction than simply grabbing an umbrella or heading for cover. What about those left in the rain, those whose lives are more impacted? This is what we are focused on in this chapter, as we continue our argument for the need for a new business climate, new forms of proactive leadership, one where the impossible is now possible.

The lessons of systems

With change a constant, leadership at all levels must be more forward-thinking and more inclusive. It is how one leads when not necessarily in charge, how one influences others regardless of one's role and how one ensures that every voice is heard. The critical part we each play is defined within a larger system of change, whether what we are trying to change is big and complex (like meeting the needs of the growing population of older adults) or broad and finite (figuring out ways for parents to help their children flourish through distance-learning during a pandemic). How we lead matters and who leads us matters even more.

What can we learn in practice from concepts such as 'systems leadership' – also called collective leadership – and how can they help us more effectively improve our communities? The World Economic Forum defines system leadership as a collective of three key elements: the individual (with collaborative leadership skills), the system (with complex systems insight) and the community (with coalition-building and advocacy tactics). These 'systems leaders', as they are called, combine many of the usual aspects of how we might define good leaders – possessing strengths centred on creating responsive organizations and frameworks, having the ability to inspire and drive change, as well as executing forward-thinking activities. 'Unlike traditional leaders, they are often humble, good listeners and skilled facilitators who can successfully engage stakeholders with highly divergent priorities and perspectives. Systems leaders see their role as catalyzing, enabling and supporting widespread action – rather than occupying the spotlight themselves.'[2]

It's also more than the ability to create consensus across more diverse groups and broader needs. These leaders have the ability to convene and commit with all stakeholders to address complex issues (getting more than their own teams on board for a change is important to their success). They understand how things are connected to one another, and how a broader perspective on addressing an issue impacts each group. They engage, energize and inspire all stakeholders and get them committed towards progressing the goals of the common good.

Systems leaders act with accountability, ensuring success is always about more than themselves. They focus on co-creating a better future and finding solutions that help meet the collective needs of every community. These leaders care about the health of the whole, build broad relationships through active listening, and build networks of trust and collaboration. This is what we saw in action time and time again in the leaders that we spoke to for *Beyond Good*: a new form of leadership that seeks context and connectivity.

The stirring of the soul within our work

Within the principles of systems leadership, one can try to map out the product of our collective labour to establish that interconnection. It's part of developing a deeper awareness of what role you play, and the type of impact your business or industry has. Alan Briskin, in his book on organizational development, *The Stirring of Soul in the Workplace*, describes what we learn about ourselves in our work: 'The honing of our capacity for experience requires something of the skills of an archaeologist, the capacity to rummage around within ourselves and pose questions about what we discover. When we plumb the depths of experience, we invariably find the connections between past events, current behaviour and future choices. We have a greater capacity to find meaning.'[3]

While connecting (or creating) meaning within our work is largely a personal journey, a number of organizations have attempted to assist their employees' efforts. Briskin sees it as a personal imperative: 'We must each wrestle with the larger purpose of our work. In a world connected with soul, our collective efforts matter. The spirit in which we do our work is intimately related to the products of others, to the service we provide to the greater community.'[4]

We are all connected organisms, and our work is simply one (important) part of that relationship. We must develop more opportunities to drive personal connections to our work and the positive impacts we can have on people's lives. But how do we really awaken the soul – this inner core value – of our work? How do we appreciate this symbiotic relationship to one another and break out of the prevailing paradigm?

Peter M Senge, proponent of systems leadership and author of *The Fifth Discipline: The art & practice of the learning organization,* defines systems thinking as 'a discipline for seeing wholes. It is a framework for seeing interrelationships rather than things, for seeing patterns of change rather than static "snapshots". It is a set of general principles... and systems thinking is a sensibility – for the subtle interconnectedness that gives living systems their unique character... Systems thinking is the antidote to this sense of helplessness that many feel.'[5] The secret is to break out of these traps, to remove these mental boundaries and move past them.

To understand the connection of our work to a greater purpose, Senge suggests we need to remove both spatial blindness (seeing the part without seeing the whole) and temporal blindness (seeing the present without seeing the past): 'reality is made up of circles, but we see straight lines.'[6] Most people feel this intrinsically – that what we do is more than a function, that it has a greater purpose. As more people are given the chance to lead and have their voices heard, we will see more societal shifts. Senge goes on to say, 'With a shared vision, we are more likely to expose our ways of thinking, give up deeply held views, and recognize personal and organizational shortcomings. All that trouble seems trivial compared with the importance of what we are trying to create. As Robert Fritz puts it, "in the presence of greatness, pettiness disappears". In the absence of a great dream, pettiness prevails.'[7] We must all not only dare to dream, but act on these dreams to drive necessary change.

We must change how we organize ourselves to realize a better future, a future which values our fellow humans first and foremost – no exceptions. The future is a choice we make together. We are human, after all. PATRICK RIVENBARK, PRINCIPAL AT THE RIVENBARK GROUP

SPOTLIGHT ON MX – A CULTURE OF PURPOSE

When we think about founding stories and culture, none stands out more than MX, a FinTech provider based in the Silicon Slopes in Utah. Its visionaries, Ryan Caldwell, Brandon Dewitt, Nate Gardner and James Dotter and many others, represent and shape the culture of the company and the *heart* of MX. It's a founding story that feels very different from a Silicon Valley one.

MX was born in 2010, shortly after the financial crisis. Its mission is to empower the world to be financially strong and to influence the financial-services industry to be different – to be better. It is a big hairy audacious goal, especially for an industry whose business model is very much based on fees. MX helps cleanse, aggregate and present financial transaction data more clearly. This enables their bank and credit-union clients help their customers and members more fully understand their financial condition and better manage their finances.

'Financial institutions have a moral imperative to always be advancing mankind, to be a guiding adviser for their customers,' says Nate Gardner, Chief Customer Officer of MX. Perhaps, not surprisingly, one of MX's core values is the Founder's Mindset:

'If not me, then who? If not now, then when?' The resolve to tackle challenges big and small is not only part of the company's DNA; it also reflects part of the team's personal character – rooted in a keen sense of putting purpose before profit, of building a strong foundation for how society should operate.

To make a purposeful contribution means focusing on something beyond the immediate financial reward, not sacrificing long-term success for short-term gains. According to James Dotter, CFO of MX, 'Success should not be solely based on a monetary yardstick; focus on purpose and creating value – redefine your goal from being a financial intermediary to becoming a true financial advocate.' For a startup, that is still partly reliant on venture capital, this can be challenging. 'You have to decide: Are you going to be a builder and executor, or will you be a handshake entrepreneur?' says Brandon Dewitt, Co-Founder & CTO at MX.

Just like having a group of employees who share the same values, having a group of investors that are aligned with the company's mission is just as crucial. What happens when you start measuring the organization's contribution to the society, to the consumers and to the industry as a whole?

In practical terms, it means having a team where you can have vigorous debates, but walk away stronger; it means having the passion to build something truly meaningful, and innovating to move mankind forward; it means having a healthy, deliberate culture to do good – one that is tightly integrated with your core values. Building something meaningful is hard work. But as the team at MX shows, it can be done, even in the modern world of data.

I don't know if we could have had the company to the degree that we did, if we didn't have these unique personalities that share the common values and desire to impact the world.

RYAN CALDWELL, FOUNDER & CEO OF MX

Technology (and investment) for social good

When we think about how systems leadership can help nurture deeper connectivity and meaning in our work, we have to talk about another type of system, one of society's greatest enablers – the ever-present weight of technology. While we've provided examples of how technology is impacting the common good, the spectre of technology in our lives and in the context of our labour is ever-present.

From the glow of always-on smartphones to the prescient ding of notifications, these particular applications of science have an inordinate impact on our daily lives and on how we perceive the future. It's no longer a case of 'can technology be leveraged for social good' but rather, 'why don't we see more applications designed for the real problems' across our communities? Surely humanity's workforce can create things of more consistent value beyond those that simply entertain. What about more creative ways to help more people? Answering that starts with venture capital, and, once again, the choices we all make – what we prioritize, where we work, and the technology and services that we choose to consume.

Foundations of the formidable

In too many foundational stories – especially those originating with technology firms in Silicon Valley, London and other cosmopolitan innovation centres – it feels like the success that we see, the end result, is always this perfect set of connected dots going backwards in time towards an upbringing that made this success inevitable. If only life were as perfect as these founding stories. What is often built in Silicon Valley or any cosmopolitan innovation centre is a reflection of its exclusion, bias and blind spots, and not necessarily a representation of the wide spectrum of needs of our communities. This is why we need new and different stories to build a different future.

Building a company purely to facilitate personal financial success shouldn't be our sole goal, but you wouldn't know it by looking at most venture investments. How much more could have been done with the talented teams that helped global technology companies become what they are? It's not just scale, riches or excess. If this is what we strive for, what our society's foundations are formed upon, then humanity is in trouble (and perhaps we are already there). We need companies to do more than sell people things, serve up ads and pry into our personal data for their own benefit.

When do we focus less on being innovative and focus more on simply being good – helping our communities and helping the people around us? When do our business models and our actions actually align with our values? We have to stop the talking and start acting in a way that demonstrates that there is more beyond ourselves and more beyond the present day.

The cost and opportunity of capital

All businesses large and small have a starting point. Many progress to a point where, as Jim Collins describes it in *Good to Great*, they develop their hedgehog – their reason for being. This creates central forces that help a company scale, fend off competition and develop a flywheel of business momentum. Increasingly, these central forces have technology at the core of their business model and often a reliance on venture-capital investment to fund their development.

Consider that more than $1.5 trillion was invested globally in venture capital deals between 2010 and 2019. In 2019 alone, according to Crunchbase,[8] roughly $294.8 billion was invested in nearly 32,800 deals. In 2018, that number was even more – $322 billion across 31,931 deals. Each one of those represented a company that received an investment pinned to the hope that a large enough percentage of those investments would have an incremental return through an exit – either an acquisition or by having their shares go public through an initial public offering (IPO).

What ideas and which founders get funded matters. As we work to shed light on business models that create more for the community, and more for the common good, the impact of bias within venture capital matters a great deal. There is a significant opportunity cost, which shows up in both which founders get funded (the majority of funders and founders are white and male) and which ideas have a chance to succeed. That these decisions are based on a certain amount of bias and pure focus on profit is important to consider, even if conditions improve.

Think about the last time you did a search on the internet for an article or an image. Chances are, when you type in 'successful entrepreneur' or 'leadership', you will see a sea of homogeneous white male faces. While we do not lack successful female leaders or entrepreneurs who are Black, Asian or Latinx, they are typically not prominently represented in the media, digital or print. Not only does this perpetuate unconscious bias for humans seeking information, this bias also creeps into automated systems and algorithms that are learning by scanning more prejudiced data, further reinforcing the discrimination against certain populations within our society. This doesn't help our community, nor the cohesiveness needed on the path forward.

Our communities also lose out when truly good ideas aren't funded because they aren't deemed profitable, or don't quite fit the model and mindset of the investor funding them. Or when the needs of marginalized communities are deemed too much of a niche for investment, even though the underlying solution is anything but. We hear this time and time again from founders from under-represented communities.

What if we focused on more incentives for businesses that enhance the financial health of their communities and really create long-term benefit for more people? Better financial services have the ability to improve lives significantly, as financial success and better financial security enhance both physical wellbeing, longevity and intergenerational success.

Those that help improve society have to be further incentivized to combat the existing transactional capitalistic model that more often profits the few at the expense of the needs of the community. Eradicating the negative impact of which ideas we fund will require thoughtful leadership, from local to national level, from private to public sectors. To develop a more inclusive business environment within our communities, we should do the following:

- Promote capital investment in minority communities and businesses.
- Promote reskilling and lifelong access to learning.
- Require increased transparency and reporting for capital investment.
- Develop tax policies that encourage more diverse entrepreneurship and stimulate local development.
- Require companies to develop mentorship programmes; be transparent on diverse talent-acquisition and pay.
- Encourage entrepreneurship as a track for education.
- Create different pathways for education and learning.
- Incentivize and invest in local innovation hubs.
- Encourage more public and private co-creation and partnerships.

Talking the talk and walking the walk

There are some bright spots on our path forward. We are seeing many companies get funded through a new wave of venture-capital firms like Flourish Ventures, whose partners or corporate sponsors focus on the greater good globally and within their communities. These companies are focused on leveraging technology to provide more services to their communities and are connecting purpose to the work their teams focus on. We are also seeing a renewal in how leadership is being defined at how our leaders are ingesting new forms of business ethics designed for a new age.

Once a self-centred bank and treasury-focused industry, FinTech has become a more outward-facing space by fostering inclusion and increasing access to financial services. MICHELE TIVEY, CO-FOUNDER, CEO AT PAYOMETRY

While purpose is the new green, this goes beyond mission statements. Organizations must be willing to check their own blind spots, follow through with their words, and execute a new vision. Here are some of the stories of those guided by this new North Star.

SPOTLIGHT ON PROJECT100

We begin with the story of Jimmy Chen, CEO of New York-based FinTech startup Propel, which helps Supplemental Nutrition Assistance Program (SNAP) users check food stamp balances via their Fresh EBT app. The devastating impact of Covid-19 on low-income families cannot be understated. About 80 per cent who work have lost significant income during this pandemic; more than half of their users report that they only have a few days of food and/or money on hand.

A few months after the onset of the pandemic in the US, while many cities were under lockdown and businesses were shattered, Propel joined forces with GiveDirectly and Stand For Children to form Project100, with a goal to raise $100 million for 100,000 families in need, identified using data from their user base.

Not only did they exceed their goal two weeks early, they have since expanded their efforts to deliver cash relief to more low-income families in need – termed Project100-Plus. It is by far the most ambitious Covid-19 private direct-payments initiative to date in the United States.

People solve problems that they understand. The reality is that people who have the means to start a new company or join a major bank and start a new initiative generally come from a certain background that is not representative of everybody in the United States, especially that of low-income Americans. JIMMY CHEN, FOUNDER AND CEO OF PROPEL

Propel's story, along with countless others, demonstrates the power of leveraging technology not only to gain efficiencies, but also to do good for our society. Propel is also one of the startups in the first cohort of Financial Solutions Lab, managed by the Financial Health Network (previously known as CFSI), in collaboration with JPMorgan Chase as founding partner. The Financial Solutions Lab's mission, according to the Financial Health Network, is to cultivate, support and scale innovative ideas that advance the financial health of low-to-moderate-income (LMI) individuals and historically underserved communities.

SPOTLIGHT ON FINANCIAL HEALTH NETWORK

Previously known as CFSI, the Financial Health Network is a non-profit organization founded in 2004, with the idea that businesses can provide responsible and high-quality financial products and services while making money at the same time. The name was changed to reflect the broader scope of financial health, beyond the financial-services sectors, to include employers, hospitals and higher-education institutions.

Over the last seven years, the Financial Solutions Lab, a $60-million, 10-year initiative managed by the Financial Health Network in collaboration with founding partner JPMorgan Chase and with support from Prudential Financial, has gone through its own evolution as well. The first five years of the Financial Solutions Lab's journey was about pushing the financial-health agenda; the focus of the next five years is on driving an inclusive recovery and

---

using FinTech and innovation as a force to help the most vulnerable people build resilience and financial health.

According to data from the Financial Solutions Lab, more than 200 not-for-profit and FinTech organizations have been selected to participate in its programmes. The Financial Solutions Lab Accelerator has, over the course of its first six years, supported more than 40 early-stage startup companies focused on financial health, reaching more than 10 million customers with their solutions, more than half of whom are low- to moderate-income. Overall, consumers have saved more than $2 billion using solutions from Financial Solutions Lab companies.

Apart from running the Accelerator Program, the Financial Solutions Lab also oversees a non-profit FinTech exchange – with more than 150 organizations – that enables non-profit and FinTech providers to explore collaboration and build high-impact partnerships. To date, the Nonprofit-FinTech Exchange has delivered more than $850,000 in grants to 16 non-profit-FinTech partnerships in an effort to build a more inclusive FinTech landscape. Some of the Financial Solutions Lab's portfolio companies include:

- **Even**
  Reduces reliance on payday loans and provides a platform to enhance consumer certainty and provide real-time information to support informed financial decisions.

- **HoneyBee**
  A service that allows employers to provide employees access to an extra week's pay interest-free, as well as financial coaching.

- **Nova Credit**
  Provides a credit-scoring solution that facilitates immigrants' access to financial services and credit without having a US-based credit history.

You cannot take action on what you cannot measure. JENNIFER
TESCHER, FOUNDER AND CEO FINANCIAL HEALTH NETWORK

Sustainability is not a spectator sport

As with diversity and inclusion, sustainability can no longer be a side issue or a slogan reserved for corporate-responsibility reports. Increasingly, sustainability is being included as part of an organization's core strategy and daily processes, as corporations are recognizing that we all have a role to play in contributing to a healthier planet. Aspiration in the US and Alipay in China show us how financial technology can be used to help us build a more sustainable and inclusive future. Here are their stories.

SPOTLIGHT ON ASPIRATION

Aspiration is a US-based FinTech and a Certified B Corporation, joining a global community of leaders to redefine success in business and to build a more inclusive and sustainable economy. Former speechwriter, policy adviser and financial fraud prosecutor, Andrei Cherny founded Aspiration as a reaction to what he saw as an opportunity to create a different kind of customer relationship and experience, with a business model focused on building trust.

In our discussion for *Beyond Good*, Cherny said, 'FinTech is a way to unlock the power of individuals to make decisions that are in line with their values.' And he's backing that up through Aspiration's transparent pricing model and more environmental-focused services. Their offering of 'pay what you think is fair' pricing is revolutionary within the industry.

Aspiration's personal-impact score gives consumers an insight into how their day-to-day decisions impact their personal goals that are in line with their values towards a more sustainable environment. With the *Plant Your Change* feature, each purchase made is rounded to the nearest whole dollar; in partnership with tree-planting charities around the world, including Eden Reforestation Projects, Aspiration plants one tree for each round-up.

This startup with a conscience is also not shy about pointing out the roles that big banks play in fossil-fuel financing. While much of Aspiration's user base mirrors that of the population in the US, what's interesting about this FinTech, compared to incumbents, is the much higher level of user engagement on social media, compared to other FinTechs and incumbent financial institutions. There is something to be said about having an engaging and passionate user community that believes in the mission of the company, and shares a sense of collective responsibility; a community that is no longer tied to geography, but one that brings people together based on their shared values. Doing good should not be a bolt-on activity, but part of the DNA of all businesses.

More people understand how their money has its own moral voice. ANDREI CHERNY, CO-FOUNDER OF ASPIRATION

SPOTLIGHT ON ANT FOREST – BY ALIPAY

Ant Forest is a mini-programme within the Alibaba superapp, introduced in 2016 as part of Alipay. Leveraging gamification and behavioural economics, it encourages its users to adopt a greener lifestyle and incentivizes low-carbon activities, such as paying utility bills online or walking to work instead of driving, by rewarding the behaviour with tree-planting initiatives. Users can view real-time aerial images of Alipay Ant Forest trees, and they can also grow them jointly with friends and family.

According to Ant Group, over 550 million people have joined the Alipay Ant Forest, planting 200 million trees in China through Alipay and its partners, reducing 12 million tons of carbon emission, creating 400,000 job opportunities for local communities and generating RMB 60 million in income as of August 2018. Doing well by doing good can come about click by click, especially in markets like China.

The programme was given the UN Champions of the Earth award[9] and the 2019 UN Global Climate Action Award. The initiative has also inspired GCash App from the Philippines to introduce GCash Forest, which enables local users to contribute to reforestation and environmental preservation by adopting a low-carbon lifestyle. If more corporations like Ant Group engaged their customers to create positive impacts on large societal problems like climate change, imagine what other issues we could tackle.

With consumers becoming more aware of the devastating impact of the climate crisis, one wonders why we have not seen an even bigger push in the industry towards Environmental, Social and Corporate Governance (ESG) and more competition with FinTechs focused on conscious consumerism. These goals, adopted and expanded as part of the United Nations Sustainable Development Goals (SDGs) as part of their 2030 Agenda for Sustainable Development, should be reviewed by all organizations, regardless of the industry, as a guide for ways their efforts can deliver even greater impact. Simon Cocking, Chief Editor of *Irish Tech News*, shares his sense of urgency with us: 'If we fail to do this we are speeding over the edge of a precipice in terms of our future existence. We don't have another planet to reboot our lifestyles on.'

Focus on sustainability should be one of the core operating principles. After all, the challenge is simply too immense for one industry sector or one group to solve. And let's be honest: no one has all the answers. But together we have a fighting chance for shared prosperity. What goals does your company hold at its core, and do they reflect your personal values? Maybe it's time for another review.

So many banks are talking, few are acting. Real change requires action and not words. This means reviewing all aspects of the banking business, and all of its investments, and rebalancing away from fossil fuel firms and those organisations creating greenhouse emissions and shifting the balance to renewables and carbon-offset schemes. More than this, it means the banks and their investors must look into their souls and ask: Are we doing the right thing? What planet are you leaving for our children? CHRIS SKINNER, CHAIRMAN – FINANCIAL SERVICES CLUB

Equal value in all lives

A society's wealth is not measured by how much equity is accumulated by individuals – or in the case of the US, the top 1 per cent. Rather, it is measured by how well its citizens watch out for one another; how it lifts up those who are the most vulnerable; and how its bonds are strengthened through the most challenging times – working towards one common purpose. We are one civilization. We share one home. It's past time that we work together and protect our future – together as one global community. One of the many organizations that embodies this spirit of togetherness is the Bill & Melinda Gates Foundation, launched in 2000, and the largest private foundation in the world.

SPOTLIGHT ON BILL & MELINDA GATES FOUNDATION AND FINANCIAL SERVICES FOR THE POOR

Core to the foundation's mission is the belief that *every life has equal value*. In developing countries, its projects focus on improving people's health and giving them the chance to lift themselves out of hunger and extreme poverty. In the United States, it seeks to ensure that all people, especially those with the fewest resources, have access to the opportunities they need to succeed in school and life.

Specifically, the Foundation's Global Growth Opportunity Program addresses challenges around infrastructure (such as access to clean water and sanitation), agriculture, gender and

---

equality, and financial services for the poor. The latter focuses on connecting 1.7 billion people to formal financial services, which can add trillions of dollars to the GDP.

According to figures from the World Bank, only 63 per cent of adults in developing economies have an account with financial institutions,[10] and women are often excluded from these beneficial financial systems, with a 9 per cent persistent gender gap in financial inclusion in developing economies. Its Level One Project, for example, helps public and private sectors develop pro-poor, digital financial services and markets towards creating an inclusive and interconnected digital economy. Some efforts include:

- **Mojaloop**
  Open-source software that can be used by any organizations to create and deploy interoperable digital-payment systems, connecting the underserved with the emerging digital economy.

- **The Africa Digital Financial Inclusion Facility (ADFI)**
  Launched with Agence Française de Développement (AFD) and the government of Luxembourg, to advance financial inclusion for at least 320 million more Africans, of which nearly 60 per cent are women. According to the African Development Bank, by 2030, the ADFI will deploy $400 million in the form of grants and affordable loans to institutions to enable digital finance.

- **G2Px Initiative**
  Launched in partnership with the World Bank, to digitize government-to-person payments. Such efforts have gained significance during Covid-19 as more governments around the world have announced plans to scale up social-assistance payments, putting cash in the hands of those who need it. With many women working in the informal sectors (95 per cent of women in Asia and 89 per cent of women in Sub-Saharan Africa, according to the World Bank), it is now more important than ever to make sure that these women are sufficiently protected and empowered.[11]

As evidenced from the months after Covid-19, digital payments gained critical prominence as withdrawing money from bank branches became more difficult. Governments worldwide, including that in the US, also needed ways to distribute relief funds efficiently to those in need. Even pre-Covid-19, the GSM Association indicated that 60 per cent of mobile-money providers reported partnering with a humanitarian organization to deliver mobile-money-enabled cash and voucher assistance to over 2.7 million unique mobile-money accounts. With technology solutions in tow, we have entered a new era of public-led digital assistance.[12]

According to the GSMA, the digitization of payments has reached new heights, with the ratio of digital-to-cash-based transactions increasing by nearly 50 per cent since 2017. The number of registered mobile-money accounts exceeded 1 billion worldwide, with over \$1.9 billion processed daily by the mobile-money industry. Mobile money is becoming increasingly integral to the global financial ecosystem, enabling growth in international remittances, crucial to the growth of developing economies. Adjacent services have developed, including access to credit, insurance and saving, which help unlock opportunities for economic growth, driving innovation and entrepreneurship, and in so doing, are helping to slowly close the gender gap within global financial services.

Purpose and profit not only must co-exist; they are actually inseparable. The question is whether we are going to build our businesses, our communities, our families and our lives for the long-term. If we continue to build for quarterly profits or short-term gain, we can't wonder why there is a fragility in the system. Building a company with the people, systems and ethics that we most desire can't be done overnight. Smart businesspeople take a much longer view – much like a farmer watering a plant long before the harvest is due. CATHERINE FLAX, MANAGING DIRECTOR, CRA, INC

From new forms of responsible banking to more sustainable business models, we can see how *even banking* can find a higher purpose. How can we be assured that the next generation of leaders will be even more open-minded, more able to focus on systems-leadership principles of serving the common good of their communities? One way is through education, especially at the highest levels.

SPOTLIGHT ON EDUCATION AND ETHICS

Having pondered economic systems and good business models in the last chapter, we also need to think about the individuals and institutions who make decisions that may result in deeper levels of inequalities. How any given society instills a sense of empathy and a shared code of ethics certainly has consequences.

While we are encouraged by the increased focus on equality and justice taught in schools for younger children, we still need to continue the effort to reshape empathy as we grow. Regardless of which industry and which company we work in, we all have a role to play in building a better future together – one that is fair, equal and sustainable. Regardless of what job function we are in – whether it's finance or engineering – it is as crucial to maximize profit and efficiency as it is to consider the social impact of decisions made personally and professionally.

'We have created a monster with the MBA that should not exist,' says Paul Polman, former Unilever boss and current chair of the Saïd Business School at Oxford. Many business leaders are suggesting that 'sustainability, purpose and social responsibility are at least as important as profit maximization.'[13] The concept of doing well while doing good should be ingrained into the fabric of life, and a focus on humanity should be as crucial as gaining technical know-how.

As more programmes are created globally to help broaden the vision of future business leaders, and as all of us become more aware of the critical roles that individuals and businesses play, we

---

can only hope that the fundamentals of stakeholder capitalism become more deeply integrated into the curriculum and our everyday lives. This is what will be required to change mindsets geared towards the longer term and focused on the common good. Every action counts.

A new path and new principles

There is a new way forward – a new path for businesses and a new form of leader for them. It is one of purpose and one focused on being connected to our community and the common good. We have taken this journey together, first discussing the shifting tides that will impact us even more in the future – longer lives with more complex needs, changes in how we work, who we work for and how companies are formed. We have shed light on the importance of multiple forms of inclusion and have reflected on the diversity of our community. We have gained a new appreciation and awareness of bias.

We have talked about how to best serve the forgotten demographics, and the importance of alternative business models that consider more than just profit, with examples from financial services to ice cream. We have discussed how we think about work and new ways to look at leadership. And we have given examples of businesses and leaders that exemplify these ideals.

Our central thesis in *Beyond Good* is that we must find deeper purpose and act upon it. Doing good shouldn't be a corporate responsibility on a PowerPoint deck or a corporate manifesto. The onus is on all of us to do what is right for our society. It is up to us to write our own narrative.

We must focus on the responsibility that we all have to engage the needs of our greater community and to demonstrate empathy towards the rest of humanity; after all, we are all connected, and each decision we make, each path we take, will impact what follows. As our good friend and former CEO of 11 FS Foundry, Dr Leda Glyptis said to us: 'If you are not empathetic and present you have failed right out of the gate.'

Our work means something more than a value exchange for money; we need to adjust our thinking and expand our mental maps to see what is beyond us. We must forge new partnerships, ones that extend beyond our silos. The challenges that we face today cannot be solved without all the stakeholders at the table: innovators, entrepreneurs, venture capitalists, educators, policy-makers and technologists; thinkers and doers; everyone who is passionate about changing the future for the better.

We have taken this journey ourselves as well, through research and conversations with leaders across the globe, across industries and business models. And across a global pandemic which still rages on and will continue beyond this publication. Through social isolation and virtual learning, through the common experience of loss and a deeper sense of community, we have forged ahead towards a deeper appreciation of our interdependency.

What we have gained through this journey is perspective, one that we have both refined through our own lens and perspectives, but also a journey influenced by you. What we have come up with results in what comes next, a core set of principles – ones that we hope can act as a guide to conversations and personal reflection.

Are *you* the kind of leader that connects purpose with a broader proximity?

Are *you* a dreamer that believes in a better world and a communal purpose?

Are *you* a believer in working towards a common good?

Then join us on this journey – one that goes *Beyond Good.*

CHAPTER NINE

Moving hearts and mindsets (to action)

We ourselves feel that what we are doing is just a drop in the ocean. But if the drop was not in the ocean, I think the ocean would be less because of the missing drop.[1] MOTHER TERESA

A different picture

As we stated at the beginning of *Beyond Good*, this is not meant to be a regular business book. Rather, it is intended to be a journey where we can explore ways towards more empathetic leadership. It is designed to get us all thinking differently about trends such as longevity and the future of work, about positive business models, the ethics of decisions and the trade-offs we make. Through the examples of individuals, organizations and leadership concepts, we have tried to create a framework within which personal and business decisions can be taken that collectively create a common good and fulfil a purpose that goes beyond ourselves.

We hope that we have helped you reframe the world a bit, as you have the opportunity and privilege to lead it. Whether you are building the minds of children or making decisions for a nation, your words, ideas and actions matter to the progress of humanity. What we do in life echoes in eternity.

This book is not meant to provide the answers to every challenge that our society is facing. Rather than completing a guide for you, we wanted to guide you through questions about the future, about where you stand in the universe and how your actions can help us all work towards a common good.

This wasn't ever going to be a complete picture, and that was partly on purpose. To spend time tearing apart a business model would be to commit to a biased point of view. To highlight one company after another without context might defeat the purpose of showing how these ideas meet a familiar focal point. To explain where you must go next – taking this step here and that one there – would be over-reaching. But to not ask you questions about your personal ethics would not be true to our values. We mean to poke, we mean to prod, we mean to find answers with you, not for you. To envision a utopia would be naive.

Every moment matters. Every action, however small, matters. We must, at all levels of leadership and working endeavour, think more deeply about the impact of our actions – and almost more importantly our inaction – on others within our communities. We must think more about the privileges that we have in life, the lottery of luck that got us here, and how to help those who we don't find to be equal. If not you, if not us, then who?

We are all part of the invisible hand now. Whether it is compensation, education, opportunity, access to very basic needs – there is always something more we can do. Thinking about our impact is not enough, we must be focused on taking action. Our lives, our local communities, and the future of our global society is at stake. Are we doing what truly matters?

Somewhere in time

Step back for a minute and reflect upon life. What does it conjure up in your mind? Now think about your life and all that surrounds you; the memories that you have created and the journeys you have taken. Our lives are relatively short and we are but a grain of sand compared to the vast expanse of the universe. What path will you be on next? Will you be a passenger, or will you chart your own course? When you hear that siren of empathy sing, how will you answer, to what will you commit?

How can we take our collective lessons of isolation – including new norms of remote work and distance learning – and create more connectivity to the needs of each other? How can we take this unprecedented moment for humanity and turn empathy and compassion into lessons of hope? Perhaps far too many of us lie dormant when we should be chasing the light, when we should be enabling the hopes and dreams and needs of one another, for in that quest we often find our own.

There's a reason we bring this up in this way – because we are coming to the end – and there is so much more to say. It is far past time to rebuild, it is far past time for action. In the end, what do we truly stand for? How did we make our mark?

A new social contract

When we speak about a new social contract, we mean a renewal of personal connectivity. We make decisions every day that impact others, whether we take time to acknowledge them or not. The values we have, the way we work and use technology, how we make decisions as consumers – they all have impact. As does the way we frame our life's purpose, regardless of the role we are able to play. The more fortunate we are, the luckier we are, the more choices we can make, the more privileged we should feel, the more thankful we should be. When we see examples of leaders incapable of showing empathy for the people around them, let alone the customers and communities they serve, this behaviour becomes more normalized and further estranges the marginalized among humanity.

The burden lies with each one of us. We must make a personal commitment to be more aware of our bias, of the barriers and unscalable ladders that face the people around us, as well as our actions to improve the lives of others less fortunate. How are we helping people to that next rung? How is our business purpose – and our personal leadership – part of our own mission to help people?

Embedding empathy (as a service)

Technology can feel like an unstoppable force, further entrenching the 1s and 0s of personal data that we simultaneously spin off and consume into the complexity of algorithms and user experiences. All of these terabytes of data are creating an unknown long-term impact on our daily lives and are leading to business models that are questionable at best and downright nefarious at worst.

While we are not advocating against technology, we should nevertheless challenge how it influences our decisions, and how bias and exclusion can creep into the ether through the wafers of silicon in our devices. Is it possible that technology's impact on the way businesses are run today is as detrimental to society as our quest for profit driving other societal inequalities? Will the harm to social fabric outweigh the benefits?

The old adage is that if something is free, we are the product. In this case, our data has been a goldmine to companies, most of which we haven't even heard of, for decades. Large technology platforms have simply made the collection and application of our data incredibly efficient and able to anticipate our desires. Social media companies, whose business models are built on engagement, are more focused on tactics that encourage clicks than being the the gatekeeper of truth, sowing the seeds for discourse and unrest. Can more types of technology be used for the greater good? Can we combine more of the ethos of the B Corporation into business models consumed by it?

As we think about our role and our work and its deep implications for society, how can we embed empathy deeper into the systems around us, whether they are of human or machine origin? This is an existential question of the near term, with implications for the long term, as humanity is losing the battle of the business model to large platforms with very muddled morals. How will technology take care of more of us, given the reality of longevity trends? How can we form real community connections when much of the social technology only divides us, taking tribalism to new depths? How can we combat the negative effects of technology to embed empathy within these black boxes that control more and more aspects of our lives? How can we ensure that algorithms care more about improving lives than selling goods and displaying ads? It comes down to people and purpose.

As artificial intelligence helps usher in the fourth industrial age, how will AI-embedded applications impact the greater society? How could leaders create a new social contract that further embeds empathy into our lives, to slowly improve the collective actions and the behaviour of humanity through new forms of smart applications that will make society stronger and more equal?

Rapid technological advances have only begun to make their impact on humanity. Businesses – especially those controlling capital such as financial institutions, or those controlling data at scale such as social technology platforms – act as both gatekeepers and enablers. These businesses and their leaders have a huge role to play. And if you are in one of these roles, listen up. While some executives may not subscribe to the dire mantra of innovate or die, their directives to their teams and their words to shareholders matter. Publicly working on infrastructure and efficiency projects to reduce costs may be signals to the equity markets that your profits will increase; but like corporate restructuring, this demonstrates a lack of imagination and a short-term view. As we said earlier, it is far past time to evaluate how your business model and future strategies will benefit not just your bottom line but that of the communities you serve.

What have you done to ensure that we have a better future? One that lasts beyond *you*?

ONE WORLD. ONE VOICE. ONE VISION

Through the research for this book, and through our One Vision podcast, alongside Arun Krishnakumar, we have been very fortunate to meet many amazing people whose stories need to be told, whose voices need to be amplified, and whose journeys offer an inspiration to so many others within our industry. Through the voices of others, we have begun to see a new narrative emerge for the role of technology, one driven by new injections of empathy, and one that looks at ways to solve existing problems within our communities through a different lens.

Ramya Joseph is the Founder and CEO of Pefin. Ramya went from working in proprietary trading at Goldman Sachs to founding the world's first AI-based financial adviser. As algorithms become increasingly instrumental in determining societal outcomes, Ramya and her team recognized that many wealth advisers – both automated and human-driven – were missing key tradeoffs that everyone makes that affect the management of wealth, impacting decisions for women, families and all investors differently. Their AI-driven platform monitors over 2 million data points about their client's financial life in real time. At the core is Ramya's belief that a more diligent understanding of personalized data should help alleviate any biases that might skew good financial outcomes.

Pefin's quest to make a dent in the financial universe is beautifully articulated by Ramya Joseph: 'AI is created by humans, for humans.'

Serial entrepreneur Hantz Févry was born in Port-au-Prince, Haiti. After attending university in New York, two earth-shattering events led him down the path to build his latest startup. The first was the 2008 economic crisis that severely impacted his home country and led him to help create online job postings from his dorm room to help Haitians at home find work. The second was experiencing the devastating January 2010 earthquake that severely disrupted his country just as he was heading back to finish school. A job at Google helped launch him on his path to found his startup Stoovo, which enables gig workers to optimize their income through a consolidated dashboard of work opportunities. Stoovo has integrations with over 1,400 providers aimed at helping transitory workers earn more from their time. Févry says, 'I believe in the progress of humanity with the help of technology.' [2]

The Co-Founder and COO of EverSafe, Liz Loewy, is the former chief of the elder abuse unit in the New York County District Attorney's Office. She knows a thing or two about prosecuting financial fraud, especially attempts to defraud older adults. Financial exploitation comes in different forms, from phishing to identity theft and romance scams by strangers and professional scammers, to close family members stealing money from joint accounts or threatening abandonment, among others. And it is a growing problem, and for Liz Loewy and her co-founder, Howard Tischler, it's a personal one. One of the reasons Howard co-founded EverSafe was that his mother was a victim of this kind of fraud. By analysing daily transactions to identify anomalies including missing deposits and late bill payments, EverSafe can help find signs of potential cognitive decline, and the likelihood of falling victim to financial exploitation. EverSafe connects designated 'trusted advocates' through alerts. For entrepreneurs like Liz and Howard, there is no mission more important than helping older people stay safe.

By working with businesses that are changing the narrative within financial services, and helping share their stories, companies like Pefin, Stoovo and EverSafe are making change contagious. By continuing our efforts to change the system from within through helping external ideas propagate, we are attempting to do the same. Our belief is that anyone with great ideas should have a chance to succeed. Marking the hundredth episode of our One Vision podcast in September 2020, we continue to leverage our voices to bolster those who work hard to change the hearts and mindsets of many. And we are grateful for those who have joined us on our journey:

At its best, FinTech has the power to provide those services to billions of people, which will have an enormous impact on the financial security and long-term opportunities for people who are being left behind. Every day that I can help push the industry towards that goal is a good day in my book. GREG PALMER, VP AT FINOVATE

FinTech's end goal is to bring greater financial inclusion to the planet and give everyone access to the financial system. I want to be part of that and say to young people, 'Hey you don't remember when you actually had to go to the bank?' RICHARD TURRIN, AUTHOR OF *INNOVATION LAB EXCELLENCE*

Over the last five years, FinTech has had a gigantic impact with firms disrupting the status quo and incumbent providers upping their game to compete. I am in this game to build better money, programmable, enabling and inclusive. CHARLES D'HAUSSY, FORMER HEAD OF FINTECH AT INVESTHK

Hearts, mindsets and action

What are the ways we must change in a world that itself is nothing but change? Let's start by improving the communities we are in by caring more for our environment. Thinking of sustainability brings to mind Apple and their commitment to a cleaner supply chain, that focuses on ensuring equitable labour practices and more refined environmental protections, including proper recycling for products at the end of their useful life. Aspiration focuses on improving the environment by helping their consumers understand their footprint through their transactions on the front end and where the company invests in on the back end. Ant Group helps consumers offset the impact of their purchases by planting trees through Ant Forest. There are countless other examples big and small.

Every consumer and every company must think more and improve upon their physical impact in their communities. What are you doing to think more about the impact of your consumption, about your environmental impact on the planet and on your community? What about the products and services your company creates? What are their long-term impacts? It is in the smallest of changes that we make the most change. Collectively, we must protect the one planet that we call home.

There are so many areas we must learn from to make better lives for others. How do we engage more of our own communities by celebrating and leveraging their diversity? From speaking up to creating space, by looking back in order to look forward, we each have a role to play – personally and professionally.

A model most changed

From the conversations we've had for *Beyond Good* and our experiences working with the financial-service and technology ecosystems, we know this once great machine is changing. What happens when banking's traditional business model becomes disconnected from its past through embedded finance, open banking and further encroachment by venture-backed startups and large technology platforms? What happens when the profit motive of banking shifts towards one that is closer to the model we espouse? Can this industry act as a beacon and build upon the good that we see – reinventing itself with purpose? Perhaps wishful thinking, yet we *persist* (and have been for over a decade) – because we must.

The financial services model of *Beyond Good* is about much more than inclusion. It means offering all functions, all features, all facets that banking offers to facilitate a better life for all, not just for some. It means systems and procedures and regulations geared towards one of equal treatment, and not one that merely pays lip service to that notion. It means continuing the momentum to fix what has not been working for many, and to add value, to create new ways to help lift up everyone in our community.

Banking itself – whether by being embedded, unbundled, bundled, made more open or simply disappearing – is changing. Slowly, but surely, we are shifting hearts and mindsets. There is much work to be done, but more and more people are joining this movement every day – to challenge the status quo and create opportunities to achieve one's dreams and aspirations, not just for oneself but for generations after. This must be our true north.

To go *Beyond Good* requires industry to reinvent its core values to ensure that every single participant is treated equally in a true representation of a marketplace designed for the benefit of all, dismantling the systemic bias and barriers erected decades ago. Through these principles we can make banking better. We can make banking *Beyond Good*. If we can do this for financial services, will your industry be next?

The fire within

At the beginning of the conversation we had around new business models we started with the company Lego and looked at how its founder, Ole Kirk Kristiansen, withstood the impact of personal family tragedies and professional setbacks, including fires that destroyed his factories several times. With his family, they rebuilt new factories and new beginnings, and started the great company Lego we know today. We talked about their modern-day commitment to sustainable manufacturing of their iconic interlocking bricks and acknowledged their pivot towards community needs and a changing environment. But their commitment to their customers and global society hasn't ended there. Looking to continue innovating – towards the principles we espouse in *Beyond Good* – their venture arm continues to push their business model forward to embrace the needs of their global community. Lego Ventures has invested in 11 startups, including Klang (exploring the future of humanity through media), PeppyPals (teaching children about emotions through pet-based toys), Thrively (which develops unique digital-lesson plans to help primary-school children thrive) and Caper (which creates on- and off-screen missions to engage children's minds).[3] Along these lines, Lego Ventures invests in four primary categories:

- **Education technology**
  Investing in education technologies and companies that can influence the way children are engaged and retained through early education. Enabling technologies should have the agility to scale globally with products that should be playful and foster curiosity, collaboration and open-ended problem-solving.

- **21st-century skill development**
  In the era of the fourth industrial revolution, Lego Ventures believes skills such as creativity, curiosity, critical thinking,

collaboration, confidence and empathy will be more important than ever before. They are looking to invest in companies that share their belief and are providing innovative offerings, focusing on developing these essential life skills.

- **New play spaces**
  Parents and children are demanding deep and immersive play experiences, which seamlessly transcend space and time while engaging the entire family.

- **Creative making**
  Both creative confidence and ability will be core attributes for the future workforce, and investments in these areas will help develop children more prepared for the future.

Their most recent investment, alongside Sesame Street-affiliated venture team, Sesame Workshop, was taking part in a $50 million investment round in Homer, an early-education startup building apps to teach literacy and other childhood skills.[4] The Lego Group is more than taking their brand to market; their investments and commitment to innovate to meet the demands of the next century of childhood learning demonstrates that their corporate values are aligned with the heart of their global community. How can we think about our industry, our company, our work and do the same? How do we keep an open mind to continue on this journey beyond these final pages?

The next stage of the journey

There are innumerable wrongs to right within our global society – in the heart of each community – but we have to stand for something, and we have to start somewhere. What we are asking is this. Be the change you want to see. Be the voice that raises your hand and asks if there is a different way, to question when things don't feel right, to demand that things be better.

Stand up, do the homework, dig up the data, pull examples from other industries, because we can assure you, they are right there in front of you.

We need to be aware of and eliminate our own biases that hold back the possibility of greater unity within our own community, so that we can rebuild our global society. We must eliminate the bias we have towards the status quo that tells us that this can't be done. We have witnessed that the impossible is possible, that we can change our society towards the arc of fairness, towards a better and broader social contract, towards a stakeholder model where all needs are considered.

We urge you to join us in taking that next step.

Be inspired. Inspire others.

Use your voice. Stand up and shout. Start a chorus of lions.

Then act. Act up. Make a good kind of trouble.

Act in the interests of those who just can't act yet.

Teach those who don't yet know how to stand up.

Speak for those who haven't yet found their voice.

Thank you for listening to ours.

Let's go beyond. *Beyond Good.*

To a place called hope.

CHAPTER TEN

Principles of *Beyond Good*

Let's take the following principles – categorized by the major themes within *Beyond Good* – to create change towards the common good in your community, within your company and through your work. Which ones might spur you to action and which ones can you also believe?

On purpose

We believe that what we do in life should create personal meaning for us, and it should somehow reflect our values and beliefs, and as we develop deeper empathy for others, our work becomes more and more connected to improving the human condition. Our success is tied to the success of others.

Towards the common good

We believe in the power of the common good, the idea that there is more to us than ourselves, and that the daily decisions we make have a ripple effect on the communities we live in and those that we are fortunate to serve through our work, through our ideas and through our actions. We are stronger together.

Embracing diversity and inclusion

We believe that every voice matters, that people should be treated equally, fairly and consistently regardless of age, gender, race, origin, sexual orientation, religion, location, education, income and wealth. We believe that economic opportunities should not be restricted to one group, and we must recognize that we all rise with an inclusive future of work.

Regarding prosperity

We believe that everyone should have equal access to the building blocks of prosperity. We must strive to create more opportunities for people to truly thrive, to create an environment without economically induced fears or setbacks. We believe that economic equality is a basic right.

Fairer financial services

We believe that the financial services industry can be a catalyst for a better society, that innovation in banking is about unlocking potentials previously deemed unattainable, and serving demographics previously considered undesirable. This will require greater transparency and a focus on more long-term relationships and value creation, rather than shorter-term profit cycles. We can create opportunities to enable society as a whole to prosper and make banking better.

Technology

We believe that all technological advances are ultimately about humans – and our quest to leverage the powerful combination of human and machine can create a more equitable future that we can all aspire to.

On empathy

We believe that empathy must be our key driver for personal and business decisions, and that we must always focus on meeting the most basic human needs by being human ourselves. We believe that inequality is a human-made problem that can be solved – and with our collective commitment we will change society for the better.

Aspiration and hope

We believe that the decisions we make in life matter, that everyone can make a difference in the communities where they live and to those that they are fortunate to serve. We believe in the power of hope, and that we must always dare to dream for a better future. This is at the heart of *Beyond Good*.

But I have not lost hope. I have not lost hope because I am persuaded again and again that, lying dormant in the deepest roots of most, if not all, cultures there is an essential similarity, something that could be made – if the will to do so existed – a genuinely unifying starting point for that new code of human co-existence that would be firmly anchored in the great diversity of human traditions.[1] VÁCLAV HAVEL

The future will always hold some uncertainty, that's the nature of days not yet written.

Thank you all for being part of our journey.

Let's write a better future – together.

References

Introduction

1 Clifford, C (7 February 2017) Ruth Bader Ginsburg says this is the secret to living a meaningful life, *CNBC*, https://www.cnbc.com/2017/02/07/ruth-bader-ginsburg-says-this-is-the-secret-to-a-meaningful-life.html (archived at https://perma.cc/B9VE-GHXL)

Chapter 1

1 Obama, Barack (5 February 2008) Feb 5 Speech, *The New York Times* https://www.nytimes.com/2008/02/05/us/politics/05text-obama.html (archived at https://perma.cc/5FCP-QCWM)
2 Collins, J (2001) *Good to Great*, 1st edn, HarperCollins, New York
3 Thiel, P and Masters, B (2014) *Zero to One*, 1st edn, Crown Publishing Group, New York
4 Collins, J and Hansen, M (2001) *Great by Choice*, 1st edn, HarperCollins, New York
5 Smith, A and Seligman, E R A (1910) *An Inquiry into the Nature and Causes of the Wealth of Nations*, J M Dent & Sons, Ltd, UK
6 Investopedia (6 January 2019) What Does the Term 'Invisible Hand' Refer to in the Economy? https://www.investopedia.com/ask/answers/011915/what-does-term-invisible-hand-refer-economy.asp (archived at https://perma.cc/EG6W-N7HL)
7 Mainwaring, S (11 August 2016) How Lego Rebuilt Itself as a Purposeful and Sustainable Brand, *Forbes*, https://www.forbes.com/sites/simonmainwaring/2016/08/11/how-lego-rebuilt-itself-as-a-purposeful-and-sustainable-brand/#58e05e816f3c (archived at https://perma.cc/5746-W8JK)
8 United Nations (2019) World Population Prospects 2019, United Nations Department of Economic and Social Affairs Population Division, New York, https://population.un.org/wpp/Publications/Files/WPP2019_Highlights.pdf (archived at https://perma.cc/RB53-9Y2S)

9　Servat, C, Super, N and Irving, P (2019) Age Forward Cities for 2030, Milken Institute Center For The Future Of Aging, Santa Monica, https://milkeninstitute.org/sites/default/files/reports-pdf/Age%20 Forward%202030_FINAL_DIGITAL_WEB_Dec%202.pdf (archived at https://perma.cc/3V4J-X82D)

10　Scott, A (2019) A Longevity Agenda for Singapore (p 6), Stanford Center on Longevity, Singapore, http://longevity.stanford.edu/wp-content/uploads/2019/11/A-Longevity-Agenda-for-Singapore.pdf (archived at https://perma.cc/JAQ3-L3KR)

11　United Nations (2019) World Population Prospects 2019, United Nations Department of Economic and Social Affairs Population Division, New York, https://population.un.org/wpp/Publications/ Files/WPP2019_Highlights.pdf (archived at https://perma.cc/RB53-9Y2S)

12　Singapore Population, Government of Singapore Department of Statistics, https://www.singstat.gov.sg/modules/infographics/ population (archived at https://perma.cc/T9VK-S9LP)

13　Apple (15 September 2020) Singapore and Apple Partner on National Health Initiative Using Apple Watch, https://www.apple.com/ newsroom/2020/09/singapore-and-apple-partner-on-national-health-initiative-using-apple-watch (archived at https://perma.cc/CBM3-B5P6)

14　SkillsFuture Singapore (22 September 2020) IBM and SkillsFuture Singapore Launch New SGUnited Programme to Train 800 Mid-career Professionals, https://www.skillsfuture.sg/NewsAndUpdates/ DetailPage/6d360d38-1b81-48c4-a85e-0daefb991682 (archived at https://perma.cc/VX38-M9FV)

15　OECD (2017) How Does Spain Compare? Preventing Ageing Unequally, p 1, https://www.oecd.org/spain/PAU2017-ESP-En.pdf (archived at https://perma.cc/MRA9-NQNN)

16　OECD/European Observatory on Health Systems and Policies (2019) Spain: Country Health Profile 2019, State of Health in the EU, pp 3–4, OECD Publishing, Paris/European Observatory on Health Systems and Policies, Brussels, https://ec.europa.eu/health/sites/health/ files/state/docs/2019_chp_es_english.pdf (archived at https://perma.cc/ ZWU9-4S88)

17 Frayer, L and Shapiro, A (16 February 2015) Not A Group House, Not A Commune: Europe experiments with co-housing, *NPR*, https://www.npr.org/sections/parallels/2015/02/16/385528919/not-a-group-house-not-a-commune-europe-experiments-with-co-housing (archived at https://perma.cc/M9EZ-ZQ5Y)

18 Grahame, A (10 October 2018) What Would an Age-friendly City Look Like?, *The Guardian*, https://www.theguardian.com/cities/2018/oct/10/what-would-an-age-friendly-city-look-like (archived at https://perma.cc/TM2M-2UKB)

19 BBC (30 January 2012) Japan Population to Shrink By One-third by 2060, https://www.bbc.com/news/world-asia-16787538 (archived at https://perma.cc/U3KQ-82B5)

20 Wamsley, L (24 December 2019) Japan's Births Decline To Lowest Number On Record, *NPR*, https://www.npr.org/2019/12/24/791132555/japans-births-decline-to-lowest-number-on-record (archived at https://perma.cc/VVP3-8F5D)

21 Toshihiro, M (6 February 2019) Japan's Historic Immigration Reform: A work in progress, *Nippon*, https://www.nippon.com/en/in-depth/a06004/japan%E2%80%99s-historic-immigration-reform-a-work-in-progress.html (archived at https://perma.cc/K5WX-GAV9)

22 World Economic Forum (2020) Global Social Mobility Index 2020: Why economies benefit from fixing inequality, https://www.weforum.org/reports/global-social-mobility-index-2020-why-economies-benefit-from-fixing-inequality (archived at https://perma.cc/6EVN-DGTP)

23 World Economic Forum (2020) Global Social Mobility Index 2020: Why economies benefit from fixing inequality, https://www.weforum.org/reports/global-social-mobility-index-2020-why-economies-benefit-from-fixing-inequality (archived at https://perma.cc/6EVN-DGTP)

24 Oxfam International (2020) Time to Care: Unpaid and underpaid care work and the global inequality crisis, https://indepth.oxfam.org.uk/time-to-care/ (archived at https://perma.cc/E9WB-S8N7)

25 Oxfam International (2020) Time to Care: Unpaid and underpaid care work and the global inequality crisis, https://indepth.oxfam.org.uk/time-to-care/ (archived at https://perma.cc/E9WB-S8N7)

26 Hait, A (13 March 2019) Rise in Self Employed Challenges the Common Wisdom, *United States Census Bureau*, https://www.census.gov/library/stories/2019/03/what-is-a-business.html (archived at https://perma.cc/AR9L-CQSY)

27 Prudential (2019) Gig Workers in America, p 2, https://www.prudential.
   com/wps/wcm/connect/4c7de648-54fb-4ba7-98de-9f0ce03810e8/
   gig-workers-in-america.pdf?MOD=AJPERES&CVID=mD-yCXo
   (archived at https://perma.cc/JVB9-MBPG)

28 Fry, R (24 July 2019) Baby Boomers are Staying in the Labor Force at
   Rates Not Seen in Generations for People Their Age, *Pew Research
   Center*, https://www.pewresearch.org/fact-tank/2019/07/24/baby-
   boomers-us-labor-force/ (archived at https://perma.cc/P7DJ-GUMQ)

29 Ozimek, A (3 October 2019) Report: Freelancing and the economy in
   2019, *Upwork*, https://www.upwork.com/press/economics/freelancing-
   and-the-economy-in-2019/ (archived at https://perma.cc/X8ER-LX2F)

30 Prudential (2019) Gig Workers in America, p 2, https://www.prudential.
   com/wps/wcm/connect/4c7de648-54fb-4ba7-98de-9f0ce03810e8/
   gig-workers-in-america.pdf?MOD=AJPERES&CVID=mD-yCXo
   (archived at https://perma.cc/JVB9-MBPG)

31 OECD (2018) Entrepreneurship at a Glance – 2018 Highlights, pp 4 &
   8 http://www.oecd.org/sdd/business-stats/EAG-2018-Highlights.pdf
   (archived at https://perma.cc/GZD7-G2XE)

32 OECD (2018) Entrepreneurship at a Glance – 2018 Highlights, pp 4 &
   8 http://www.oecd.org/sdd/business-stats/EAG-2018-Highlights.pdf
   (archived at https://perma.cc/GZD7-G2XE)

33 PwC/CB Insights (2020) MoneyTree Report, Venture Capital Funding
   Report Q2, pp 46–7, https://www.cbinsights.com/research/report/
   venture-capital-q2-2020/ (archived at https://perma.cc/3ZGG-CFSF)

34 PwC/CB Insights (2020) MoneyTree Report, Venture Capital Funding
   Report Q2, pp 46–7, https://www.cbinsights.com/research/report/
   venture-capital-q2-2020/ (archived at https://perma.cc/3ZGG-CFSF)

35 Startup Genome (2020) The Global Startup Ecosystem Report 2020,
   pp 27–8, https://startupgenome.com/all-reports (archived at https://
   perma.cc/8VSF-MZHH)

36 Startup Genome (2020) The Global Startup Ecosystem Report 2020,
   pp 27–8, https://startupgenome.com/all-reports (archived at https://
   perma.cc/8VSF-MZHH)

37 Hwang, V (2019) Saving Main: Betting big on small, Kauffman
   Foundation, https://youtu.be/vhlf4MKEqDI?t=161 (archived at
   https://perma.cc/BA8P-ULCG)

38 World Economic Forum (2019) Global Gender Gap Report 2020, pp 5–6, Mind the 100 Year Gap, Geneva, Switzerland, https://www.weforum.org/reports/gender-gap-2020-report-100-years-pay-equality (archived at https://perma.cc/X8AS-M73S)

39 World Economic Forum (2019) Global Gender Gap Report 2020, pp 5–6, Mind the 100 Year Gap, Geneva, Switzerland, https://www.weforum.org/reports/gender-gap-2020-report-100-years-pay-equality (archived at https://perma.cc/X8AS-M73S)

40 World Economic Forum (2019) Global Gender Gap Report 2020, pp 5–6, Mind the 100 Year Gap, Geneva, Switzerland, https://www.weforum.org/reports/gender-gap-2020-report-100-years-pay-equality (archived at https://perma.cc/X8AS-M73S)

41 Fry, R (20 June 2019) US Women Near Milestone in the College-educated Labor Force, *Pew Research Center Fact Tank*, https://www.pewresearch.org/fact-tank/2019/06/20/u-s-women-near-milestone-in-the-college-educated-labor-force/ (archived at https://perma.cc/A48H-PQPA)

42 Catalyst (2 December 2020) Women CEOs of the S&P 500, https://www.catalyst.org/research/women-ceos-of-the-sp-500/ (archived at https://perma.cc/R78A-J92A)

43 Lu, D, Huang, J, Seshagiri, A, Park, H, and Griggs,T (9 September 2020) Faces of Power: 80% are white, even as US becomes more diverse, *The New York Times*, https://www.nytimes.com/interactive/2020/09/09/us/powerful-people-race-us.html (archived at https://perma.cc/685N-PKJX)

44 Ewing-Nelson, C (2020) Four Times More Women Than Men Dropped Out of the Labor Force in September, *National Women's Law Center,* https://nwlc-ciw49tixgw5lbab.stackpathdns.com/wp-content/uploads/2020/10/september-jobs-fs1.pdf (archived at https://perma.cc/6XHV-42HE)

45 Madgavkar, A, Manyika, J, Krishnan, M, Ellingrud, K, Yee, L, Woetzel, J, Chui, M, Hunt, V and Balakrishnan, S (2019) The Future of Women at Work: Transitions in the age of automation, *McKinsey Global Institute*, p 1, https://www.mckinsey.com/featured-insights/gender-equality/the-future-of-women-at-work-transitions-in-the-age-of-automation (archived at https://perma.cc/5CT7-U99N)

Chapter 2

1 Angelou, M (1993) *Wouldn't Take Nothing for My Journey Now*, 1st edn, Random House Publishing Group, New York

2 Jackson, A (29 August 2017) The 10 most serious problems in the world, according to millennials, *Business Insider*, https://www.businessinsider.com/world-problems-most-serious-according-to-millennials-2017-8 (archived at https://perma.cc/H6TA-99SA)

3 World Bank, Poverty Overview, https://www.worldbank.org/en/topic/poverty/overview (archived at https://perma.cc/2MY2-95ZH)

4 Balestra, C and Tonkin, R (2018) Inequalities in Household Wealth Across OECD Countries: Evidence from the OECD Wealth Distribution Database, *OECD Statistics Working Papers*, No. 2018/01, p 38, OECD Publishing, Paris, https://doi.org/10.1787/7e1bf673-en (archived at https://perma.cc/7NQ8-ABQT)

5 Partington, R (14 May 2019) Britain Risks Heading to US Levels of Inequality, Warns Top Economist, *The Guardian*, https://www.theguardian.com/inequality/2019/may/14/britain-risks-heading-to-us-levels-of-inequality-warns-top-economist (archived at https://perma.cc/9SWM-HBNX)

6 Collins, C, Ocampo, O, and Paslaski, S (2020) Billionaire Bonanza 2020: Wealth windfalls, tumbling taxes, and pandemic profiteers, *Institute for Policy Studies*, p 1, https://inequality.org/great-divide/billionaire-bonanza-2020/ (archived at https://perma.cc/PNZ7-W9S9)

7 Inequality.org, Global Inequality, https://inequality.org/facts/global-inequality/ (archived at https://perma.cc/Y5MD-H3DF)

8 Shorrocks, A, Davies, J and Lluberas, R (2019) Global Wealth Report 2019, *Credit Suisse Research Institute*, pp 5 & 13, https://www.credit-suisse.com/about-us/en/reports-research/global-wealth-report.html (archived at https://perma.cc/X5MW-A7FH)

9 Shorrocks, A, Davies, J and Lluberas, R (2019) Global Wealth Report 2019, *Credit Suisse Research Institute*, pp 5 & 13, https://www.credit-suisse.com/about-us/en/reports-research/global-wealth-report.html (archived at https://perma.cc/X5MW-A7FH)

10 UN Women (2018) Turning Promises into Action: Gender equality in the 2030 Agenda for Sustainable Development', SDG monitoring report, *UN Women*, New York, pp 2 & 5, https://www.unwomen.org/en/digital-library/sdg-report (archived at https://perma.cc/MH4T-WUCN)

11 Shontell, A and Akhtar, A (9 May 2019) Women spend 7 more years working than men and get no money or credit for it, *Business Insider*, https://www.businessinsider.com/melinda-gates-unpaid-work-women-men-2019-5 (archived at https://perma.cc/AA7G-GR7R)

12 Oxfam International (2020) Time to Care: Unpaid and underpaid care work and the global inequality crisis', p 10, https://indepth.oxfam.org.uk/time-to-care/ (archived at https://perma.cc/E9WB-S8N7)

13 World Bank (19 April 2018) Financial Inclusion on the Rise, But Gaps Remain, Global Findex Database Shows, https://www.worldbank.org/en/news/press-release/2018/04/19/financial-inclusion-on-the-rise-but-gaps-remain-global-findex-database-shows (archived at https://perma.cc/3CUR-HCGK)

14 FAO, IFAD, UNICEF, WFP and WHO (2020) The State of Food Security and Nutrition in the World 2020, Transforming food systems for affordable healthy diets, pp 3 & 23, http://www.fao.org/3/ca9692en/online/ca9692en.html (archived at https://perma.cc/2GK4-J5X4)

15 Food and Agricultural Organization of the United Nations (2020) Tracking progress on food and agriculture-related SDG indicators 2020, http://www.fao.org/sdg-progress-report/en/ (archived at https://perma.cc/J2YA-V9FU)

16 FAO, IFAD, UNICEF, WFP and WHO (2020) The State of Food Security and Nutrition in the World 2020, Transforming food systems for affordable healthy diets, pp 3 & 23, http://www.fao.org/3/ca9692en/online/ca9692en.html (archived at https://perma.cc/2GK4-J5X4)

17 UN-Water, Water, Sanitation and Hygiene, https://www.unwater.org/water-facts/water-sanitation-and-hygiene/ (archived at https://perma.cc/3MG7-582R)

18 UN-Water, Water, Sanitation and Hygiene, https://www.unwater.org/water-facts/water-sanitation-and-hygiene/ (archived at https://perma.cc/3MG7-582R)

19 United Nations (2019) World Population Prospects 2019: Highlights, p 1, United Nations Department of Economic and Social Affairs, Population Division, New York, https://population.un.org/wpp/Publications/Files/WPP2019_Highlights.pdf (archived at https://perma.cc/RB53-9Y2S)

20 National Institution for Transforming India (2019) Composite Water Management Index, New Delhi, pp 27 & 29, https://niti.gov.in/sites/default/files/2019-08/CWMI-2.0-latest.pdf (archived at https://perma.cc/YE8P-966A)

21 National Institution for Transforming India (2019) Composite Water Management Index, New Delhi, pp 27 & 29, https://niti.gov.in/sites/default/files/2019-08/CWMI-2.0-latest.pdf (archived at https://perma.cc/YE8P-966A)

22 PwC/CB Insights (2020) MoneyTree Report Venture Capital Funding Report Q2 2020, p 46, https://www.cbinsights.com/research/report/venture-capital-q2-2020/ (archived at https://perma.cc/3ZGG-CFSF)

23 Atkinson, R, Muro, M and Whiton, J (9 December 2019) The Case For Growth Centers: How to spread tech innovation across America, *Brookings*, https://www.brookings.edu/research/growth-centers-how-to-spread-tech-innovation-across-america/ (archived at https://perma.cc/5RYG-AFGL)

24 Dougherty, C (29 December 2019) California Is Booming. Why are so many Californians unhappy?, *The New York Times*, https://www.nytimes.com/2019/12/29/business/economy/california-economy-housing-homeless.html (archived at https://perma.cc/EU3K-LQ53)

25 Farha, L (2018) Report of the Special Rapporteur on adequate housing as a component of the right to an adequate standard of living, and on the right to non-discrimination in this context, *General Assembly of the United Nations*, http://www.undocs.org/A/73/310/rev.1 (archived at https://perma.cc/XB76-HJSH)

26 Lenhart, A, Swenson, H, and Schulte, B (12 December 2019) Navigating Work And Care: Struggling to balance work and care, *New America*, https://www.newamerica.org/better-life-lab/reports/navigating-work-and-care/ (archived at https://perma.cc/838D-WAYR)

27 Dow, D M (2019) *Mothering While Black: Boundaries and burdens of middle-class parenthood*, University of California Press, Oakland

28 UN Women (2018) Turning Promises into Action: Gender equality in the 2030 Agenda for Sustainable Development', SDG monitoring report, *UN Women*, New York, pp 2 & 5, https://www.unwomen.org/en/digital-library/sdg-report (archived at https://perma.cc/MH4T-WUCN)

29 Gates, M (15 July 2020) The Pandemic's Toll on Women: Covid-19 is gender-blind, but not gender-neutral, *Foreign Affairs*, https://www.foreignaffairs.com/articles/world/2020-07-15/melinda-gates-pandemics-toll-women (archived at https://perma.cc/QYA9-QRQN)

30 Citigroup (2020) Closing the Racial Inequality Gaps, Citi GPS: Global perspectives and solutions, pp 22 & 34, https://ir.citi.com/NvIUklHPilz14Hwd3oxqZBLMn1_XPqo5FrxsZD0x6hhil84ZxaxEuJUWmak51UHvYk75VKeHCMI%3D (archived at https://perma.cc/T4U9-VBRT)

31 Citigroup (2020) Closing the Racial Inequality Gaps, Citi GPS: Global perspectives and solutions, pp 22 & 34, https://ir.citi.com/NvIUklHPilz14Hwd3oxqZBLMn1_XPqo5FrxsZD0x6hhil84ZxaxEuJUWmak51UHvYk75VKeHCMI%3D (archived at https://perma.cc/T4U9-VBRT)

32 OECD/European Union (2019) The Missing Entrepreneurs 2019: Policies for inclusive entrepreneurship, OECD Publishing, Paris, https://doi.org/10.1787/3ed84801-en (archived at https://perma.cc/Q8V5-XWDR)

Chapter 3

1 Keller, H and Updike, D B (1903) *Optimism: An essay*, p 56, T Y Crowell, Germany

2 World Bank (2018) The Global Findex Database 2017, pp 4, 39–40 & 124, https://globalfindex.worldbank.org/ (archived at https://perma.cc/EJK2-FLNT)

3 World Bank (2018) The Global Findex Database 2017, pp 4, 39–40 & 124, https://globalfindex.worldbank.org/ (archived at https://perma.cc/EJK2-FLNT)

4 World Bank (2018) The Global Findex Database 2017, pp 4, 39–40 & 124, https://globalfindex.worldbank.org/ (archived at https://perma.cc/EJK2-FLNT).

5 Reuters (3 April 2019) M-Pesa helps drive up Kenyans' access to financial services, https://www.reuters.com/article/kenya-banking/m-pesa-helps-drive-up-kenyans-access-to-financial-services-study-idUSL8N21L2HK (archived at https://perma.cc/P886-BG8H)

6 Quartz (5 October 2019) Mobile-based lending is a double-edged sword in Kenya – helping but also spiking personal debt, https://qz.com/africa/1722613/mobile-money-lending-in-kenya-helps-but-also-spikes-debt/ (archived at https://perma.cc/8PXN-9D84)

7 World Bank (2018) The Global Findex Database 2017, pp 4, 39–40 & 124, https://globalfindex.worldbank.org/ (archived at https://perma.cc/EJK2-FLNT)

8 World Economic Forum (2019) Global Gender Gap Report 2020, Mind the 100 Year Gap, Geneva, Switzerland, p 12, https://www.weforum.org/reports/gender-gap-2020-report-100-years-pay-equality (archived at https://perma.cc/X8AS-M73S)

9 FDIC (2018) Share of US Households without a Bank Account Continues to Drop, https://www.fdic.gov/news/press-releases/2018/pr18077.html (archived at https://perma.cc/Z8GH-U88N)

10 Financial Health Network (2020) US Financial Health Pulse 2020 Trends Report, Chicago, Illinois, pp 5 & 14, https://finhealthnetwork.org/research/u-s-financial-health-pulse-2020-trends-report/ (archived at https://perma.cc/ZDQ6-SP4Z)

11 Financial Health Network (2020) US Financial Health Pulse 2020 Trends Report, Chicago, Illinois, pp 5 & 14, https://finhealthnetwork.org/research/u-s-financial-health-pulse-2020-trends-report/ (archived at https://perma.cc/AB9P-N95F)

12 Gov.UK (2019) Financial inclusion report 2018 to 2019, HM Treasury Department for Work & Pensions, p 4, https://www.gov.uk/government/publications/financial-inclusion-report-2018-to-2019 (archived at https://perma.cc/8EEC-67ZA)

13 FINCA, The Challenge: Alleviating Poverty through Lasting Solutions, https://finca.org/why-finca/finca-challenge/ (archived at https://perma.cc/4L82-3LD9)

14 World Bank, Universal Financial Access 2020, https://ufa.worldbank.org/ (archived at https://perma.cc/3HUR-ZB52)

15 World Bank, Financial Inclusion: Financial inclusion is a key enabler to reducing poverty and boosting prosperity, https://www.worldbank.org/en/topic/financialinclusion/overview (archived at https://perma.cc/JZ8D-MJT3)

16 World Bank, Financial Inclusion: Financial inclusion is a key enabler to reducing poverty and boosting prosperity, https://www.worldbank.org/en/topic/financialinclusion/overview (archived at https://perma.cc/JZ8D-MJT3)

17 Friedman, M (13 September 1970) The Social Responsibility of Business Is to Increase Its Profits, *The New York Times*, https://www. nytimes.com/1970/09/13/archives/a-friedman-doctrine-the-social-responsibility-of-business-is-to.html (archived at https://perma.cc/ 5PK7-39U9)

18 Paypal, About us, https://www.paypal.com/webapps/mpp/about (archived at https://perma.cc/P5SR-3NGR)

19 Mangalindan, JP (25 September 2017) PayPal CEO: It's expensive to be poor, *Yahoo Finance*, https://finance.yahoo.com/news/paypal-ceo-expensive-poor-221202508.html (archived at https://perma.cc/ U23L-7M5B)

20 Kauflin, J (15 October 2020) PayPal CEO Dan Schulman Explains His Strategy For Investing In Employees' Financial Health', *Forbes*, https://www.forbes.com/sites/jeffkauflin/2020/10/15/paypal-ceo-dan-schulman-explains-his-strategy-for-investing-in-employees-financial-health/#9c30dfd1528b (archived at https://perma.cc/NP9K-QCBN)

21 Skinner, G and Clemence, M (18 September 2019) It's a fact, scientists are the most trusted people in world, *Ipsos*, https://www.ipsos.com/ en/its-fact-scientists-are-most-trusted-people-world (archived at https://perma.cc/HR26-2DT4)

22 Accenture (11 November 2015) Banks have a $380 Billion Market Opportunity in Financial Inclusion, https://newsroom.accenture.com/ news/banks-have-a-380-billion-market-opportunity-in-financial-inclusion-accenture-and-care-international-uk-study-find.htm (archived at https://perma.cc/35NL-T74M)

Chapter 4

1 Strange, A (21 January 2020) Every Company Will Be a Fintech Company, *Andreessen Horowitz*, https://a16z.com/2020/01/21/ every-company-will-be-a-FinTech-company/ (archived at https:// perma.cc/DKC5-BQLB)

2 Bruno, P, Denecker, O, and Niederkorn, M (2020) *Accelerating Winds of Change in Global Payments,* The 2020 McKinsey Global Payments Report, *McKinsey & Company*, p 7, https://www.mckinsey.com/ industries/financial-services/our-insights/accelerating-winds-of-change-in-global-payments (archived at https://perma.cc/KMP7-A46Q)

3 CB Insights (2020) The State Of Fintech Q2'20 Report: Investment & sector trends to watch, https://www.cbinsights.com/research/report/fintech-trends-q2-2020/ (archived at https://perma.cc/68MJ-UPFG)

4 EY (2019) Global FinTech Adoption Index 2019, p 7, https://www.ey.com/en_us/ey-global-fintech-adoption-index (archived at https://perma.cc/VMV6-F8G5)

5 CB Insights (2020) The State Of Fintech Q2'20 Report: Investment & sector trends to watch, https://www.cbinsights.com/research/report/fintech-trends-q2-2020/ (archived at https://perma.cc/68MJ-UPFG)

6 Lane, E (2020) Consumer and Wealth Management, Investor Day 2020, *Goldman Sachs*, p 3, https://www.goldmansachs.com/investor-relations/investor-day-2020/ (archived at https://perma.cc/4KCU-LRVX)

7 BBVA (2020) Group BBVA 2Q20 Results, p 6, https://shareholdersandinvestors.bbva.com/financials/ (archived at https://perma.cc/T7S6-ZS2Y)

8 Ensor, B (2019) BBVA Tops Forrester's 2019 Global Mobile Banking App Reviews, *Forrester*, https://go.forrester.com/blogs/bbva-tops-forresters-2019-global-mobile-banking-app-reviews/ (archived at https://perma.cc/GDD2-MU7N)

9 BBVA (6 February 2020) Customer Net Promoter Scores Continued Upward Growth For BBVA USA's Global Wealth Team in 2019, https://www.bbva.com/en/customer-net-promoter-scores-continued-upward-growth-for-bbva-usas-global-wealth-team-in-2019/ (archived at https://perma.cc/8ZU8-A4SE)

10 CB Insights (2020) The State Of Fintech Q2'20 Report: Investment & sector trends to watch, https://www.cbinsights.com/research/report/fintech-trends-q2-2020/ (archived at https://perma.cc/68MJ-UPFG)

11 World Bank (19 April 2018) Financial Inclusion on the Rise, But Gaps Remain, Global Findex Database Shows, https://www.worldbank.org/en/news/press-release/2018/04/19/financial-inclusion-on-the-rise-but-gaps-remain-global-findex-database-shows (archived at https://perma.cc/KE2C-EM8B)

12 Grab, Grab Corporate Profile, https://assets.grab.com/wp-content/uploads/media/Grab_CompanyProfile_May2020_final.pdf (archived at https://perma.cc/J7RB-RJXW)

13 Carandang, B (13 June 2019) How FinTech is Setting Southeast Asia's SMEs Free', *World Economic Forum Agenda*, https://www.weforum.org/agenda/2019/06/fintech-is-driving-financial-inclusion-in-southeast-asia/ (archived at https://perma.cc/ZTT5-JC9G)

14 Yoon, S and Hillyer, M (16 June 2020) These are the World Economic Forum's Technology Pioneers of 2020, *World Economic Forum*, https://www.weforum.org/agenda/2020/06/technology-pioneers-2020/ (archived at https://perma.cc/F67G-AXJA)

15 Lau, T and Akkaraju, U (12 November 2019) When Algorithms Decide Whose Voices Will Be Heard, *Harvard Business Review*, https://hbr.org/2019/11/when-algorithms-decide-whose-voice-will-be-heard (archived at https://perma.cc/XG7K-4NUT)

16 Desjardins, J (17 April 2019) How much data is generated each day?, *World Economic Forum Agenda*, https://www.weforum.org/agenda/2019/04/how-much-data-is-generated-each-day-cf4bddf29f/ (archived at https://perma.cc/6K58-QSLB)

17 CB Insights (2020) The Fintech 250: The top Fintech companies of 2020, https://www.cbinsights.com/research/report/fintech-250-startups-most-promising/ (archived at https://perma.cc/RL5C-CRV2)

18 Nelson Mandela Foundation, Education Initiatives, https://www.nelsonmandela.org/content/page/nm100-education (archived at https://perma.cc/G5KM-U8MJ)

Chapter 5

1 New York Times, The (20 June 1932) Einstein is Terse in Rule For Success, p 17, https://timesmachine.nytimes.com/timesmachine/1932/06/20/100766197.html?pageNumber=17 (archived at https://perma.cc/Y7PY-38X6)

2 Betterment (2018) Gig Economy and The Future of Retirement, https://www.betterment.com/uploads/2018/05/The-Gig-Economy-Freelancing-and-Retirement-Betterment-Survey-2018_edited.pdf (archived at https://perma.cc/48Z7-9RHW)

3 Business Wire (27 April 2020) MYbank Served Over 20 Million SMEs as of 2019, Further Spurring the Growth of China's Small and Micro Businesses, https://www.businesswire.com/news/home/ 20200427005353/en/ (archived at https://perma.cc/79P2-EQ3J)

4 Ant Group (1 July 2020) Demystifying the SME Loans Operator, Ant Group's MYbank', *Medium*, https://medium.com/alipay-and-the-world/demystifying-the-sme-loans-operator-ant-groups-mybank-9c556c375a6 (archived at https://perma.cc/4ZTA-64RJ)

5 WeBank (30 April 2020) WeBank Annual Report 2019, p 9, https:// stdd.webankcdn.net/epss/upload/www/pdf/annual_report_2019_en. pdf (archived at https://perma.cc/8PFR-5BEU)

6 Tencent (9 January 2020) WeChat Mini Programs Showcases New Capabilities to Celebrate its Third Anniversary, https://www.tencent. com/en-us/articles/2200946.html (archived at https://perma.cc/ Z2LN-UV8J)

7 Google & Temasek/Bain, e-Conomy SEA 2019, *Google*, pp 4 & 45, https://www.blog.google/documents/47/SEA_Internet_Economy_ Report_2019.pdf (archived at https://perma.cc/J96A-B6M8)

8 Google & Temasek/Bain, e-Conomy SEA 2019, *Google*, pp 4 & 45, https://www.blog.google/documents/47/SEA_Internet_Economy_ Report_2019.pdf (archived at https://perma.cc/J96A-B6M8)

9 AARP (2019) The Longevity Economy Outlook, p 4, https://www. aarp.org/content/dam/aarp/research/surveys_statistics/econ/2019/ longevity-economy-outlook.doi.10.26419-2Fint.00042.001.pdf (archived at https://perma.cc/YE5W-4CPF)

10 Cohn, D and Passel, J (5 April 2018) A Record 64 Million Americans Live in Multigenerational Households, *Pew Research Center*, https:// www.pewresearch.org/fact-tank/2018/04/05/a-record-64-million-americans-live-in-multigenerational-households/ (archived at https:// perma.cc/3GCY-3LHR)

11 Rosenbloom, S (2 November 2006) Here Come the Great-Grandparents, *The New York Times*, https://www.nytimes.com/2006/11/02/fashion/ 02parents.html (archived at https://perma.cc/TU23-MYJW)

12 Azoulay, P, Jones, B F, Kim, J D and Miranda, J (11 July 2018) Research: The Average Age of a Successful Startup Founder Is 45, *Harvard Business Review*, https://hbr.org/2018/07/research-the-average-age-of-a-successful-startup-founder-is-45 (archived at https:// perma.cc/VF2Z-8M8Z)

13 Office of Financial Protection for Older Americans (February 2019) Suspicious Activity Reports on Elder Financial Exploitation: Issues and Trends, *Consumer Financial Protection Bureau*, https://files. consumerfinance.gov/f/documents/cfpb_suspicious-activity-reports-elder-financial-exploitation_report.pdf (archived at https://perma.cc/ N5R5-QZ2V), p 8

14 Cohn, D and Passel, J (5 April 2018) A Record 64 Million Americans Live in Multigenerational Households, *Pew Research Center*, https:// www.pewresearch.org/fact-tank/2018/04/05/a-record-64-million-americans-live-in-multigenerational-households/ (archived at https:// perma.cc/9W6U-3VKN)

15 Andriotis, A (2 February 2019) Over 60, and Crushed by Student Loan Debt, *Wall Street Journal*, https://www.wsj.com/articles/ over-60-and-crushed-by-student-loan-debt-11549083631 (archived at https://perma.cc/NY9L-2ESB)

16 Irving, P, Beamish, R and Burstein, A (12 June 2019) Silver to Gold: The business of aging, *Milken Institute*, https://milkeninstitute.org/ reports/silver-gold-business-aging (archived at https://perma.cc/ E9GE-9Q69)

17 United Nations (2015) World Population Ageing, p 1, https://www. un.org/en/development/desa/population/publications/pdf/ageing/ WPA2015_Highlights.pdf (archived at https://perma.cc/2FEQ-HWAZ)

18 Credit Suisse (10 October 2019) Gender Diversity is Good for Business, https://www.credit-suisse.com/about-us-news/en/articles/ news-and-expertise/cs-gender-3000-report-2019-201910.html (archived at https://perma.cc/3CSU-6EYU)

19 Women Who Code (30 March 2020) Women Who Code Equal Pay Day Report, https://www.womenwhocode.com/blog/women-who-code-equal-pay-day-report (archived at https://perma.cc/TL4E-3Q6R)

20 Peterson, D and Mann, C (September 2020) Closing the Racial Inequality Gaps: The economic cost of racial inequality in the US, p 7, *Citi,* https://www.citivelocity.com/citigps/closing-the-racial-inequality-gaps/ (archived at https://perma.cc/5NNP-55YY)

21 Catalyst (31 January 2020) Too Few Women of Color on Boards: Statistics and solutions, https://www.catalyst.org/research/women-minorities-corporate-boards/ (archived at https://perma.cc/4ANT-LHZT)

22 Mathur, P (8 October 2020) Quarterly VC Funding For Female Founders Drops to Three-year Low, *PitchBook*, https://pitchbook.com/news/articles/vc-funding-female-founders-drops-low (archived at https://perma.cc/74RK-CHA5)

23 Village Capital, 10 Years of Impact, https://vilcap.com/results (archived at https://perma.cc/DF2D-CGTS)

24 Sunrise Banks (2020) Social Impact: Community involvement, https://sunrisebanks.com/social-impact/community-involvement/ (archived at https://perma.cc/G3D3-DZ8T)

Chapter 6

1 Eu, G T (18 March 2015) Dreams Change the World, Not Technology: Jack Ma, *Digital News Asia*, https://www.digitalnewsasia.com/startups/dreams-change-the-world-not-technology-jack-ma (archived at https://perma.cc/T2FU-6YRN)

2 Shorrocks, A, Davies, J and Lluberas, R (2019) Global Wealth Report 2019, *Credit Suisse Research Institute*, p 2, https://www.credit-suisse.com/about-us/en/reports-research/global-wealth-report.html (archived at https://perma.cc/X5MW-A7FH)

3 Boushey, H (2019) *Unbound: How inequality constricts our economy and what we can do about it*, Harvard University Press, Cambridge Massachusetts

4 Inequality.org, Global Inequality, https://inequality.org/facts/global-inequality/ (archived at https://perma.cc/5RCS-3WMW)

5 Boushey, H (2020) Vision 2020: Evidence for a stronger economy, Washington Center for Equitable Growth, p 226, https://equitablegrowth.org/wp-content/uploads/2020/02/v2020-book-forweb.pdf (archived at https://perma.cc/CH7A-VZWW)

6 Samans, R (22 January 2018) A New Way to Measure Economic Growth and Progress, *World Economic Forum Agenda*, https://www.weforum.org/agenda/2018/01/towards-a-new-measure-of-growth/ (archived at https://perma.cc/9ZLM-FYJ2)

7 Mishel, L and Kandra, J (18 August 2020) CEO Compensation Surged 14% in 2019 to $21.3 Million: CEOs now earn 320 times as much as a typical worker, *Economic Policy Institute*, https://www.epi.org/publication/ceo-compensation-surged-14-in-2019-to-21-3-million-ceos-now-earn-320-times-as-much-as-a-typical-worker/ (archived at https://perma.cc/WS2E-XTWL)

8 B Corp, Certified B Corporation, https://bcorporation.net/ (archived at https://perma.cc/W4YR-6QL9)

9 Tony's Chocolonely, Annual FAIR Report 18–19, https://tonyschocolonely.com/us/en/annual-fair-reports/annual-fair-report-18-19 (archived at https://perma.cc/P7K9-FZG6)

10 California Credit Union League, The Credit Union Movement, https://ccul.org/about-us/credit-union-movement (archived at https://perma.cc/6AZC-6DBK)

11 National Credit Union Administration, *NCUA 2019 Annual Report*, https://www.ncua.gov/files/annual-reports/annual-report-2019.pdf (archived at https://perma.cc/N6SF-H4LJ)

12 World Council of Credit Unions (2018) 2018 Statistical Report, https://www.woccu.org/our_network/statreport (archived at https://perma.cc/67AD-NTDX)

13 Building Societies Association, About the BSA, https://www.bsa.org.uk/about-us/about-us (archived at https://perma.cc/Q33U-PCPM)

14 Inman, P (28 September 2008) How Turning Into Banks Led To Ruins, *The Guardian*, https://www.theguardian.com/business/2008/sep/29/bradfordbingley.creditcrunch (archived at https://perma.cc/5BLL-A9YW)

15 Omidyar Network and Oliver Wyman (2018) Breaking New Ground In FinTech, A Primer on Revenue Models That Create Value and Trust, https://www.omidyar.com/insights/breaking-new-ground (archived at https://perma.cc/CWX3-PAZW)

Chapter 7

1 Gates, H L and Wells, I B (2014) *The Light of Truth: Writings of an anti-lynching crusader*, Penguin Publishing Group, United States

2 Joint Center for Political and Economic Studies, Expand Internet Access Among Black Households, https://jointcenter.org/expand-internet-access-among-black-households/ (archived at https://perma.cc/2K5H-F2YK)

3 Essence (14 May 2020) ESSENCE Releases 'Impact Of Covid-19 On Black Women' Study, https://www.essence.com/health-and-wellness/essence-covid-19-black-women-study/ (archived at https://perma.cc/6A38-RR2N)

4 Herold, B (10 April 2020) The Disparities in Remote Learning Under Coronavirus (in Charts), *Education Week*, https://www.edweek.org/ew/articles/2020/04/10/the-disparities-in-remote-learning-under-coronavirus.html (archived at https://perma.cc/YC3Y-EVMN)

5 Obama, President Barack (14 January 2015) Remarks by the President on promoting community broadband, *The White House*, https://obamawhitehouse.archives.gov/the-press-office/2015/01/14/remarks-president-promoting-community-broadband (archived at https://perma.cc/7S7B-D2S3)

6 Canadian Radio-television and Telecommunications Commission (2020) Communications Monitoring Report 2019, p 20, https://crtc.gc.ca/pubs/cmr2019-en.pdf (archived at https://perma.cc/WU6F-G6VB)

7 Bhawan, M and Marg, J (20 August 2020) Consultation Paper on Roadmap to Promote Broadband Connectivity and Enhanced Broadband Speed, *Telecom Regulatory Authority of india (TRAI)*, p 78, https://www.trai.gov.in/sites/default/files/Broadband_CP_20082020.pdf (archived at https://perma.cc/P72D-ZW3T)

8 Sapkal, R, Chikte, A and Sengupta, U (5 June 2020) India's Digital Divide, *India Legal*, https://www.indialegallive.com/special-story/indias-digital-divide/ (archived at https://perma.cc/GVP4-SX85)

9 Watts, T and Sardone, M (30 July 2020) Creative Ideas to Support Working Parents During the Caregiver Crisis, *Mercer*, https://www.mercer.us/our-thinking/healthcare/creative-ideas-to-support-working-parents-during-the-caregiver-crisis.html (archived at https://perma.cc/V9AD-V6CS)

10 Georgieva, K, Fabrizio, S, Lim, C H and Tavares, M M (21 July 2020) The Covid-19 Gender Gap, *IMF Blog*, https://blogs.imf.org/2020/07/21/the-covid-19-gender-gap/ (archived at https://perma.cc/3TRD-PJ33)

11 Singer-Velush, N, Sherman, K and Anderson, E (15 July 2020) Microsoft Analyzed Data on Its Newly Remote Workforce, *Harvard Business Review*, https://hbr.org/2020/07/microsoft-analyzed-data-on-its-newly-remote-workforce (archived at https://perma.cc/R6J6-JA3P)

12 Kramer, S (12 December 2019) US Has World's Highest Rate of Children Living in Single-Parent Households, *Pew Research Center*, https://www.pewresearch.org/fact-tank/2019/12/12/u-s-children-more-likely-than-children-in-other-countries-to-live-with-just-one-parent/ (archived at https://perma.cc/A4TP-S5XU)

13 Smith, B (30 June 2020) Microsoft launches initiative to help 25 million people worldwide acquire the digital skills needed in a Covid-19 economy, *The Official Microsoft Blog*, https://blogs.microsoft.com/blog/2020/06/30/microsoft-launches-initiative-to-help-25-million-people-worldwide-acquire-the-digital-skills-needed-in-a-covid-19-economy/ (archived at https://perma.cc/JA7C-SYFA)

14 Foundation For The Carolinas (2017) *The Charlotte-Mecklenburg Opportunity Task Force Report*, p. 1, https://www.fftc.org/sites/default/files/2018-05/LeadingOnOpportunity_Report.pdf (archived at https://perma.cc/2692-BB8J)

15 Charlotte Digital Inclusion Alliance, Digital Inclusion Playbook, p 15, https://www.charlottedigitalinclusionalliance.org/playbook.html (archived at https://perma.cc/7CXY-9CX3)

16 Federal Communications Commission (2019) 2019 Broadband Deployment Report, p 2 https://docs.fcc.gov/public/attachments/FCC-19-44A1.pdf (archived at https://perma.cc/S32W-XQW2)

17 Kahan, J (8 April 2019) It's Time For a New Approach For Mapping Broadband Data to Better Serve Americans, *Microsoft On The Issues*, https://blogs.microsoft.com/on-the-issues/2019/04/08/its-time-for-a-new-approach-for-mapping-broadband-data-to-better-serve-americans/ (archived at https://perma.cc/8PSC-QAPL)

18 Inequality.org (18 September 2020) Updates: Billionaire Wealth, US Job Losses and Pandemic Profiteers, *Billionaire Bonanza 2020 Updates*, https://inequality.org/billionaire-bonanza-2020-updates/ (archived at https://perma.cc/UPR4-Z9E6)

19 Mishel, L and Kandra, J (18 August 2020) CEO Compensation Surged 14% in 2019 to $21.3 Million, *Economic Policy Institute*, https://www.epi.org/publication/ceo-compensation-surged-14-in-2019-to-21-3-million-ceos-now-earn-320-times-as-much-as-a-typical-worker/ (archived at https://perma.cc/WS2E-XTWL)

20 Flourish Ventures (2020) The Digital Hustle: Gig worker financial lives under pressure – Brazil spotlight, pp 3–6, https://flourishventures.com/wp-content/uploads/2020/06/Flourish-Ventures-Gig-Worker-Study-Brazil-Spotlight.pdf (archived at https://perma.cc/GM4T-BAYJ)

21 Ehrbeck, T, Gupta, H, Klemperer, S and Ramachandran, A (2020) The Digital Hustle: Gig worker financial lives under pressure – India spotlight, *Flourish Ventures*, pp 3–8, https://flourishventures.com/wp-content/uploads/2020/09/FlourishVentures-india-gig-worker-research-September-2020.pdf (archived at https://perma.cc/A5ZX-2KL9)

22 Aggarwal, S, Ehrbeck, T and Klemperer, S (2020) The Digital Hustle: Gig worker financial lives under pressure – Indonesia spotlight, *Flourish Ventures*, pp 3–5, https://flourishventures.com/wp-content/uploads/2020/09/Flourish-Ventures-Digital-Hustle-Gig-Worker-Indonesia-2020.pdf (archived at https://perma.cc/CW7R-9TY8)

23 Office of Advocacy (30 January 2019) Small Businesses Generate 44 Percent of US Economic Activity, *US Small Business Administration*, https://advocacy.sba.gov/2019/01/30/small-businesses-generate-44-percent-of-u-s-economic-activity/ (archived at https://perma.cc/9XVM-NM5N)

24 Mills, C and Battisto, J (2020) Double Jeopardy: Covid-19's Concentrated Health and Wealth Effects in Black Communities, *Federal Reserve Bank of New York*, p 2, https://www.newyorkfed.org/medialibrary/media/smallbusiness/DoubleJeopardy_Covid19andBlackOwnedBusinesses (archived at https://perma.cc/NZK4-L25L)

25 Austin, A (20 April 2016) The Color of Entrepreneurship: Why the racial gap among firms costs the US billions, *Center for Global Policy Solutions*, http://globalpolicysolutions.org/report/color-entrepreneurship-racial-gap-among-firms-costs-u-s-billions/ (archived at https://perma.cc/6EL9-JZCN)

26 Krishnakumar, A (2020) *Quantum Computing and Blockchain in Business: Exploring the applications, challenges, and collision of quantum computing and blockchain*, Packt Publishing, UK

Chapter 8

1 Senge, P M (2010) *The Fifth Discipline: The art & practice of the learning organization*, pp 68, 73 & 209, Crown, United States

2 Dreier, L, Nabarro, D and Nelson, J (24 September 2019) Systems Leadership Can Change the World – But What Exactly Is It? *World Economic Forum*, https://www.weforum.org/agenda/2019/09/systems-leadership-can-change-the-world-but-what-does-it-mean/ (archived at https://perma.cc/287T-76PB)

3 Briskin, A (1998) *The Stirring of Soul in the Workplace*, p 92, Berrett-Koehler Publishers, United States

4 Briskin, A (1998) *The Stirring of Soul in the Workplace*, p 143, Berrett-Koehler Publishers, United States

5 Senge, P M (2010) *The Fifth Discipline: The art & practice of the learning organization*, p 68, Crown, United States

6 Senge, P M (2010) *The Fifth Discipline: The art & practice of the learning organization*, p 73, Crown, United States

7 Senge, P M (2010) *The Fifth Discipline: The art & practice of the learning organization*, p 209, Crown, United States

8 Rowley, J (8 January 2020) The Q4/EOY 2019 Global VC Report: A Strong End To A Good, But Not Fantastic, Year, *Crunchbase*, https://news.crunchbase.com/news/the-q4-eoy-2019-global-vc-report-a-strong-end-to-a-good-but-not-fantastic-year/ (archived at https://perma.cc/M2HK-4CJG)

9 UN Environment Programme (19 September 2019) Chinese Initiative Ant Forest Wins UN Champions of the Earth Award, https://www.unenvironment.org/news-and-stories/press-release/chinese-initiative-ant-forest-wins-un-champions-earth-award (archived at https://perma.cc/6UNT-V7W8)

10 Bill & Melinda Gates Foundation (1998) *Financial Services for the Poor: Strategy Overview* https://www.gatesfoundation.org/What-We-Do/Global-Growth-and-Opportunity/Financial-Services-for-the-Poor (archived at https://perma.cc/2C6X-HZ7H)

11 Bull, G L, Grown, C, Guermazi, B, Rutkowski, M, Uttamchandani, M (19 August 2020) Building Back Better Means Designing Cash Transfers For Women's Empowerment, *World Bank Blogs*, https://blogs.worldbank.org/voices/building-back-better-means-designing-cash-transfers-womens-empowerment (archived at https://perma.cc/MDH5-G2E2)

12 Naghavi, N (2020) State of the Industry Report on Mobile Money 2019, *GSMA*, https://www.gsma.com/sotir/wp-content/uploads/2020/03/GSMA-State-of-the-Industry-Report-on-Mobile-Money-2019-Full-Report.pdf (archived at https://perma.cc/2HFQ-F49G)

13 Jack, A (23 February 2020) MBA Students and Employers Demand 'Profitable Solutions for People and Planet', *Financial Times*, https://www.ft.com/content/c4be5690-3b91-11ea-b84f-a62c46f39bc2 (archived at https://perma.cc/F8KU-AQBH)

Chapter 9

1 Le Joly, E and Chaliha, J (1998) *Reaching Out in Love: Stories told by Mother Teresa*, Penguin Books, London

2 Martinetti, C (July 22 2020) Hantz Févry of Stoovo: My Life As a Twenty-Something Founder, https://medium.com/authority-magazine/hantz-f%C3%A9vry-of-stoovo-my-life-as-a-twenty-something-founder-88046feadd0c (archived at https://perma.cc/76A4-TTV6)

3 LEGO Ventures, Portfolio, https://legoventures.com/portfolio/ (archived at https://perma.cc/V9L5-2PHT)

4 Business Wire (30 September 2020) HOMER, a BEGiN Brand, Raises $50 Million From LEGO Ventures, Sesame Workshop and Gymboree Play & Music, https://www.businesswire.com/news/home/20200930005232/en/HOMER-a-BEGiN-Brand-Raises-50-Million-From-LEGO-Ventures-Sesame-Workshop-and-Gymboree-Play-Music (archived at https://perma.cc/5T2H-RTC8)

Chapter 10

1 Havel, V (12 May 1995) Radical Renewal of Human Responsibility, Harvard University Commencement Speech, *humanity.org*, http://www.humanity.org/voices/commencements/vaclav-havel-harvard-university-speech-1995 (archived at https://perma.cc/4SSQ-E45G)

Index